English Simplified

An Elementary Course for Foreign Students

Hugo's Language Books Ltd

First published 1983
Second edition 1988

© 1983, 1988 Hugo's Language Books Ltd
All rights reserved
ISBN 0 85285 125 1

This impression 1989

Written by
R. F. Hanson M.A.

Illustrations by Juliet Stanwell Smith

Set in Plantin 110
Printed and bound in Great Britain by
Courier International Ltd, Tiptree, Essex

Preface

This book is a valuable and necessary learning text for any student of English. It presumes that you have an elementary knowledge of the language, and that you wish to improve it. 'Students' would include the businessman whose position requires that he be able to converse or conduct his business meetings in English. It also includes those who are working in England, whether on a temporary or permanent basis, who do not have English as a mother tongue.

Each grammatical term and concept is fully explained with particular attention paid to verb formation. (The irregular verbs at the end of the book provide you with an immediate and handy checklist.) The first section shows you how to use the present tenses (I *am*, you *are* eating) but it also deals with adverbs of frequency (*always, often, some*), possessive forms using the 'apostrophes' (the lady's hat) and comparatives (the brother is *older than* his sister). The exercises which follow each of these points ensure that you practise continually all that you have just learnt; for example, an exercise on possessive forms will include further practice on the present tenses.

The second section introduces the past tenses (I *was*, he *had been* eating), including the use of the past tense which denotes habit (they *used to* dance). Reflexive pronouns (*myself, herself*) are dealt with at this stage. Next come the future tenses (they *will* go, they *will be* going), including the strangely worded 'future in the past' (she *was going* shopping, but she decided not to). The following section gives the construction of the infinitive (*to* love) and the gerund (lov*ing*) as well as showing how modal verbs are used (i.e. sentences with 'must' or 'have to' in them, which shows that an action is necessary).

The rest of the book covers parts of speech (prepositions, clauses, etc) and how to use them, reported or indirect speech, and also the indefinite and definite articles (*as/an* and *the*). There is an extensive piece on adjectives and adverbs which will help you rapidly to improve upon the quality of English that you speak and write. This is followed by common conversational phrases (e.g. would you like . . .?) and also 'question tags' (e.g. I am pretty, *aren't I?*, you were good, *weren't you?*), so that the emphasis shifts to the spoken word – the important, idiomatic speech patterns in daily use.

The ability to speak English well, with a good accent and attention to detail regarding intonation and stress on particular words, is naturally the wish of most students. With this in mind, we have produced cassette recordings of selected extracts from 'English Simplified' which greatly enhance the course as a whole without being essential to it. However, the serious student would be well advised to ask us for further details of these tapes; our address is on the back of this book.

The author, Frank Hanson, is well equipped to write a text such as this, as he has lectured in EFL studies in both Brazilian and English colleges. Throughout the book the stress is on *self*-tuition and each part is clearly written with drawings and explanations to support that aim. 'English Simplified' is exactly what the title states: it is written simply but contains all that the foreign visitor or student needs to know about the English language.

Contents

Introduction

Sandra:	Hello! I'm Sandra. It's nice to meet you. What's your name?
Akemi:	Akemi.
Sandra:	Welcome to England. What country do you come from?
Akemi:	I come from Japan.
Sandra:	Meet my family. This is my mother

This is my father   This is my grandfather

This is my brother Derek

Have you a big family, Akemi?

Akemi:	Yes, I have a mother, a father, five brothers and three sisters.
Sandra:	Are you a student?
Akemi:	Yes I am. I'm studying English. Tell me about your English book for home study, please.
Sandra:	Here it is.
Akemi:	Is it difficult?
Sandra:	No, it's very easy, really. First you need a comfortable chair.

You also need a pen,

an exercise book,

and a good dictionary.

Akemi:	Of course! Don't I need a teacher?

Sandra: No, you don't. But it is a good idea to work with a friend.
Work for one hour every day.
Do all the exercises; it's very important.

Akemi: Show me how to do this first exercise, please.

Sandra: Yes, of course. Like this:

> ——   means you write one word
> —— —— means you write two words

For example, this question and answer . . .

> Have you a big family?   Yes, I ——— a mother, a
> father, ——— brothers and
> —— ———.
>
> Yes, I *have* a mother, a
> father, *five* brothers and
> *three sisters.*

Akemi: Are the answers in the book?

Sandra: Yes, all the answers are on page 118.

Akemi: My main problem is grammar.

Sandra: The book makes the grammar clear and easy for you.
There is a list of teaching words on page 116.

Akemi: That's good. One more thing; what about pronunciation?

Sandra: That's no problem if you buy the cassette recordings that go with
the book.

Akemi: Thank you very much for your help.
I think I'm ready to start now.

Sandra: Good luck! Enjoy your lessons. And have a lovely time in Britain.

The present tenses

The present continuous tense

This is the tense for actions happening *now*, *at the moment*.
Here is the form with the verb 'walk':

I am (= I'm) you are (= you're) he is, she is, it is (= he's, she's, it's) we are (= we're) they are (= they're)	walking

Use the forms in brackets (I'm, you're, etc) in conversation.

Question forms

am I are you is he, is she, is it are we are they	walking?

Negative forms

I'm not you aren't he, she, it isn't we aren't they aren't	walking

Note: The dog is walking
The child is walking
Mr Brown is walking

The dogs are walking
The children are walking
Mr and Mrs Brown are walking

Remember . . . Verbs ending in e (shave, smoke, write) drop that e when the
present participle ending -ing is added:

I am shaving, I am smoking, I am writing

Verbs with one vowel only and one consonant following it change also, by
doubling the consonant:

cut   I am cutting
swim   I am swimming
run   I am running

Verbs with *two* vowels followed by a consonant do not change:

speak   I am speaking
meet   I am meeting

EXERCISE 1

Look at the picture and copy the questions and answers below. Write one word for each empty space (___).

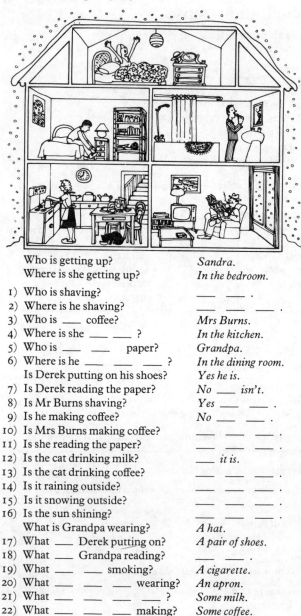

	Who is getting up?	*Sandra.*
	Where is she getting up?	*In the bedroom.*
1)	Who is shaving?	___ ___ .
2)	Where is he shaving?	___ ___ ___ .
3)	Who is ___ coffee?	*Mrs Burns.*
4)	Where is she ___ ___ ?	*In the kitchen.*
5)	Who is ___ ___ paper?	*Grandpa.*
6)	Where is he ___ ___ ___ ?	*In the dining room.*
	Is Derek putting on his shoes?	*Yes he is.*
7)	Is Derek reading the paper?	*No ___ isn't.*
8)	Is Mr Burns shaving?	*Yes ___ ___ .*
9)	Is he making coffee?	*No ___ ___ .*
10)	Is Mrs Burns making coffee?	___ ___ ___ .
11)	Is she reading the paper?	___ ___ ___ .
12)	Is the cat drinking milk?	___ *it is.*
13)	Is the cat drinking coffee?	___ ___ ___ .
14)	Is it raining outside?	___ ___ ___ .
15)	Is it snowing outside?	___ ___ ___ .
16)	Is the sun shining?	___ ___ ___ .
	What is Grandpa wearing?	*A hat.*
17)	What ___ Derek putting on?	*A pair of shoes.*
18)	What ___ Grandpa reading?	___ ___ .
19)	What ___ ___ smoking?	*A cigarette.*
20)	What ___ ___ ___ wearing?	*An apron.*
21)	What ___ ___ ___ ___ ?	*Some milk.*
22)	What ___ ___ ___ making?	*Some coffee.*

EXERCISE 2

Look at the picture here, of Mrs Burns
shouting to her husband Bill upstairs;
read what she says to him, and his reply.
Then read the questions she asks other
people in the house, and fill in the
empty spaces for their answers.

Mrs Burns:	Breakfast is ready. Hurry up, it's eight o'clock now. What are you doing, Bill? Are you coming downstairs?
Mr Burns:	No, I'm shaving.
Mrs Burns:	What are you doing, Derek? Are you shaving?
Derek:	No, ___ ___ ___ ___ ___ .
Mrs Burns:	What are you doing, Sandra? Are you putting on your shoes?
Sandra:	No, ___ ___ ___ .
Mrs Burns:	What are you doing, Grandpa? Are you getting up?
Grandpa:	No, ___ ___ ___ paper.
Mrs Burns:	Are you smoking too?
Grandpa:	Yes, ___ ___ .
Mrs Burns:	Are you smoking a pipe?
Grandpa:	No, ___ ___ ___ cigarette. What are you doing? Are you making some tea for breakfast?
Mrs Burns:	No, I'm not.
Grandpa:	What are you making then?
Mrs Burns:	___ ___ ___ coffee and it's already boiling.

EXERCISE 3

Now here are some questions for you.

1) What are you doing at the moment? (Answer: *I'm studying English*)
2) Are you standing up or sitting down?
3) Where are you sitting? (. . . in the dining room? . . . in the kitchen?)
4) What are you sitting on?
5) Are you using a pen or pencil?
6) Are you smoking?
7) What are you wearing?
8) Is it raining outside?

The present simple tense

Use this to say what happens *every day*, *always*, and *at certain times*. Here is the form with the verb 'eat'.

I you we they the dogs my brothers	eat

he she it the dog my brother	eats

Question forms:

do	I you we they the dogs my brothers	eat?

does	he she it the dog my brother	eat?

Negative forms:

I you we they the dogs my brothers	don't eat

he she it the dog my brother	doesn't eat

EXAMPLES: You eat a meal.
She eats a sandwich.
Does the dog eat a bone?
They don't eat. (They do not eat.)
I *clean* my teeth every morning.
Do you *play* football on Saturdays?
Mr Burns *doesn't have* lunch at home.

EXERCISE 4   Answer these questions like this:

What does a butcher sell?   *He sells meat.*
What do bus-conductors sell?   *They sell tickets.*

1) What does a baker sell?
2) What does a pianist play?
3) What does a footballer play?
4) What does a postman deliver?
5) What does a milkman deliver?
6) What do tobacconists sell?
7) What do pilots fly?
8) What do window-cleaners do?
9) What do ambulance-men drive?

Adverbs of frequency

Here is a list of the important adverbs of frequency:

> always
> usually/generally/normally
> often
> sometimes
> occasionally
> hardly ever/seldom/rarely
> never

Look at these sentences:

It *always* snows in Canada.   = every winter
It *usually* snows in Scotland.   = 18 winters out of 20
It *often* snows in Ireland.   = 12 winters out of 20
It *sometimes* snows in London.   = 5 winters out of 20
It *hardly ever* snows in Portugal = 1 winter out of 20
It *never* snows in Jamaica.   = 0

These words go *before* the verb ('I *always* get up at 6.30 in the morning') but they go *after* a special verb and the verb 'to be' ('He doesn't *often* smoke. He is *always* late').

EXERCISE 5

Change the sentences in Exercise 5 by using one of the above adverbs.
For example:
     Sandra goes dancing four times a week. = *She often goes dancing.*

1) Grandpa smokes a pipe every night after dinner. = *He* ___ ___ ___
   ___ ___ ___.

2) Mrs Burns goes to the cinema about once a year. = *She* ___ ___ ___
   ___ ___ ___.

3) Policemen wear uniforms all the time. = *They* ___ ___ ___.
4) Tom watches television every night except Saturday = *He* ___ ___ ___.
5) The Queen wears her crown about twice a year. = *She* ___ ___ ___ ___.
6) We go to a restaurant about once a fortnight. = *We* ___ ___ ___ ___ ___.

Remember . . . Words with a consonant + y at the end change like this:

carry – he carr*ies*   study – she stud*ies*

Words ending with –ch, –sh, –x, –s change like this:
watch – he watch*es*   push – she push*es*
fix   – Bob fix*es*   miss – Jane miss*es*

What do the Burns family do every morning after breakfast?

Read this about Mr Burns. Then copy it down. In Exercise 6, write down the same for Mr Burns and the others, changing the words in *italics* for those in the 'timetable' below. Alter 'he' to 'she' where necessary.

Mr Burns is *a businessman*. He always *takes his car out of the garage* at about 8.30 and *drives to work*. He usually *arrives at his office* at nine o'clock. At ten o'clock he generally *makes some telephone calls* and at eleven o'clock he often *has a meeting with his boss*. He *has lunch in a restaurant* at one o'clock and *seldom gets back home before seven o'clock*.

Mrs Burns a housewife	*Derek* a mechanic	*Sandra* a pupil at school	*Grandpa* retired
does the washing-up . . . tidies up the house	gets on his bike . . . rides off to work	goes out . . . catches a bus	goes outside . . . does some gardening
makes the beds	arrives at the garage	starts her classes	has a cigarette
goes shopping	repairs cars	has a music lesson	goes for a walk
visits a friend	has a tea-break	buys some sweets	meets a friend
has a snack lunch	has some sandwiches	has lunch in the school canteen	goes to a pub for lunch
usually gets home before four o'clock	sometimes gets home at six o'clock	always gets home at a quarter past four	rarely gets back home before half past five

EXERCISE 6
1) Mrs Burns is *a housewife*. She always *does the washing-up* at ___
2) Derek is ___
3) Sandra is ___
4) Grandpa is ___

Now do the same for *yourself*:
I am a ___   I always ___

There is/there are

This form is used to give facts and information:

Singular

there is there's there isn't	a	cake on the plate

but the question form of this will invert the phrase:

is there	a	cake on the plate?

Note that you must put a question mark after this form.

Plural

there are	some	cakes on the plate

but remember that *some* changes to *any* after 'not/n't' and in questions:

there aren't are there	any any	cakes on the plate cakes on the plate?

Here are some facts about Britain; copy them down and then give the same facts about your own country.

In Britain . . .
1) There is a Queen.
2) There isn't a President.
3) There are about 56 million people.
4) There are some rivers.
5) There aren't any deserts.
6) There are some very old universities.
7) There is a famous clock called Big Ben.
8) There aren't any dangerous animals.

In my country . . .
There is (There isn't) a Queen.

Very important:
Some nouns are *countable* nouns – this means that they can be counted or go with numbers, e.g.: *one* animal, *two* cats, *six* dogs

Here is a list of words that will help you to give the idea of number if you are not sure exactly how many there are.

a	→	flower (= one flower)
some	→	flowers (= more than one)
a few	→	flowers (= more than one, but not many)
many	→	flowers (= lots, i.e. more than a few)
how many	→	flowers? (= question form)

Some nouns are *uncountable* nouns – this means that they cannot be counted separately, that it is impossible to count them, e.g.: water, music, meat
Here is a list of words that will help you to describe uncountable nouns.

some	→	wine (= not a lot, not a little, somewhere in between)
a little	→	wine (= not much)
much	→	wine (= a lot of)
how much	→	wine? (= question form)

Note that in the question form *many* and *much* must be used, e.g.:
  How *many* flowers?
  How *much* wine?
It should also be used after 'not', e.g.:
  There are *not many* flowers
  There is*n't much* wine
In positive sentences use *a lot of*, e.g.:
  There is definitely *a lot of* beer left.

You will hear people ask for 'three coffees' or 'three lagers'. 'Coffee' and 'lager' are uncountable nouns but this is a short way of saying 'three *cups of* coffee' or 'three *pints of* lager'.

Look at the words in the two lists:

A

	soup
there's a little	butter
there is	milk
there isn't much	bread
there's not much	money

B

	tins
there are a few	pounds of butter
	bottles
there aren't many	loaves of bread
————————	dollars

EXERCISE 7

Where do these words go – in list A or list B? For example, *sugar* goes in List A because we say 'There's a little sugar' or 'There isn't much sugar'.

sugar; beer; cars; children; rice; cigarettes; tobacco; bottles of wine; people; cheese; sausages; petrol; spaghetti; tea; cups of tea.

Mrs Burns:	I'm going shopping. Do we need any eggs?
Sandra:	I don't know, Mummy.
Mrs Burns:	Have a look in the fridge, please.

Mrs Burns:	Are there any eggs?
Sandra:	Yes there are.
Mrs Burns:	How many are there?
Sandra:	Only three. We need some more.
Mrs Burns:	Is there any milk?
Sandra:	Only a little.
Mrs Burns:	How much cheese is there?
Sandra:	About a pound.
Mrs Burns:	We don't need any more, then. What else is there? (= *what other things*)
Sandra:	There are two bottles of beer, half a chicken and a chocolate pudding.
Mrs Burns:	Is there any fish?
Sandra:	No there isn't.

Grandpa:	I think we need some tobacco.
Mrs Burns:	No we don't!
Grandpa:	But there isn't any.
Mrs Burns:	Yes there is. It's in the dining-room.

Mr Burns:	We need some beer. There isn't any.
Sandra:	Yes there is. There are two bottles in the fridge.
Mr Burns:	That's not enough. We need some more.

EXERCISE 8 Have a look in the cupboard above. What can you see inside?
There is some salt and there ___ ___ ___ , ___ ___ and ___ ___ .
There ___ four tins ___ ___ and a packet of ___ .

EXERCISE 9 Copy and complete these sentences, in the same way as the
examples given, and using the picture as a guide:
    There isn't much milk in the fridge. *There is only a little.*
    There aren't any eggs. *There are only a few.*
1) ___ ___ ___ beer. *There* ___ ___ ___ ___ .
2) ___ ___ ___ tomatoes. *There* ___ ___ ___ ___ .
3) ___ ___ ___ bread. *There's* ___ ___ ___ .
4) ___ ___ ___ sausages. *There* ___ ___ ___ ___ .
    How much sugar is there in the cupboard? *There is a pound.*
    How many tins of soup are there? *There are four.*
5) How many eggs are there in the fridge? ___ ___ ___ .
6) How much ___ ___ ___ ___ ___ ___ ? There is about a pound.
7) ___ ___ milk ___ ___ ___ ___ ___ ? There is only a little.
8) ___ ___ bottles of beer ___ ___ ___ ___ ___ ? There are two.
9) ___ ___ fish ___ ___ ___ ___ ___ ? There isn't any.
10) ___ ___ tomatoes ___ ___ ___ ___ ___ ? There aren't any.

EXERCISE 10 Write down two things the Burns family need to buy, and two
things they do not need to buy.

EXERCISE 11
    Is there any rice? *Yes there is.*

1) Is there any sugar?   ___ ___ ___ .
2) Is there any bread?   ___ ___ ___ .
3) Is there any beer?   ___ ___ ___ .
4) Is there any spaghetti?   ___ ___ ___ .
5) Are there any onions?   ___ ___ ___ .
6) Are there any tomatoes?   ___ ___ ___ .
7) Are there any sausages?   ___ ___ ___ .
8) Are there any tins of soup? ___ ___ ___ .
9) Are there any cigarettes?   ___ ___ ___ .

Possessive forms

 This hat belongs to a cowboy. It is a cowboy's hat.

  These hats belong to cowboys. They are cowboys' hats.

See how possession by one person is shown by *'s*, whereas by two or more people it is shown by *s'*. This latter form is not used if the plural does not end in *s*; use *'s*, as in one child's toy, two children's toys.

EXERCISE 12

1) This hat belongs to an old lady. It is an old lady's ___ .

These hats belong to old ladies. They are old ladies' hats.

2) This helmet belongs to a policeman. It's ___ ___ ___ .

___ helmets ___ ___ policemen. They are policemen's ___ .

3) This hat ___ ___ ___ clown. It is ___ ___ hat.

These hats ___ ___ clowns. They ___ ___ ___ .

4) That helmet belongs to an astronaut. It's an astronaut's helmet.

Those helmets ___ ___ ___ . They are ___ ___

5) That crown ___ ___ the Queen. ___ the Queen's crown.

6) Those hats ___ ___ sailors. They ___ ___ ___ .

7) Whose hat is this? It's ___ ___ .

8) Whose hat is that? ___ ___ old lady's.

9) Whose helmets are these? ___ ___ the policemen's.

10) Whose __ __ __ ? They are the sailors'.

11) Whose hat is that, the cowboy's or the clown's? __ __ .

Copy these sentences:
a) This is my hat. = It's mine. = It belongs to me.
b) That is your hat. = It's yours. = It belongs to you.
c) That's his helmet. = It's his. = It belongs to him.
d) That's the old lady's hat. = It's hers. = It belongs to her.
e) These are our hats. = They're ours. = They belong to us.
f) Those are the sailors' hats. = They're theirs. = They belong to the sailors.

EXERCISE 13
Copy in the same way:
1) This is Helen's car.   =   __ __ .   __ __ __ __ .
2) This is our house.   =   __ __ .   __ __ __ __ .
3) That's your umbrella.   =   __ __ .   __ __ __ __ .
4) Those are his gloves.   =   __ __ .   __ __ __ __ .
5) These are my boots.   =   __ __ .   __ __ __ __ .
6) This is their farm.   =   __ __ .   __ __ __ __ .

Simple questions

Inspector: Whose file is that?
Sergeant: A man called Stubbs.
Inspector: What is his Christian name? (= his first name)
Sergeant: Bert.
Inspector: How old is he?
Sergeant: He's fifty-eight.
Inspector: What does he look like?
Sergeant: He has short hair and he is ugly.
Inspector: Is he married?
Sergeant: No, he's single.
Inspector: What's his job?
Sergeant: He hasn't got a job. He's a thief.
Inspector: What kind of thief is he?
Sergeant: He's a burglar.
Inspector: Where was he born?
Sergeant: In Liverpool.
Inspector: Where does he live?
Sergeant: He lives in Preston.
Inspector: How far is that from London?

Sergeant:	It's about 200 miles.
Inspector:	Is the form signed?
Sergeant:	Yes it is.
Inspector:	What day is it signed?
Sergeant:	29th November 1982.

Name: Bert Stubbs
Age: 58
Status: Single
Occupation: None
Address: 2 Factory Road,
　　　　　Preston, Lancashire
Place of Birth: Liverpool
Date: 29/11/82
Signature:

Bert Stubbs

EXERCISE 14

Bert has a brother called Joe. He is also a thief; he's a bank-robber. Look at the
police file on Joe, and then write down the Inspector's questions and the
Sergeant's replies as above – but using Joe's file for the answers.

Name: Joe Stubbs
Age: 60
Status: Married
Occupation: None
Address: 3 Dock Lane,
　　　　　Dublin, Ireland
Place of birth: Manchester
Date: 10/9/81
Signature:

Joe Stubbs

Can/can't, + simple present

Can is a special verb; it is often used to show *ability*, in conjunction with another verb that takes the simple present tense.

> I *can* swim = I *know how to* swim.
> She *can't* cook = She *doesn't know how to* cook.

The police think they can't catch Joe. Why not? Because . . .
Joe is a very clever bank-robber –

> He can climb walls;
> he can also climb down from high windows.
> He can open locked doors;
> he can open safes, too.
> He can run fast;
> he can drive, as well.

But the police are sure they can catch Bert.

> He isn't very clever.
> He can't drive;
> he can't run very fast, either.

Notice the words *also, too, as well, either*.
When used with 'can', these words all mean that the subject can (or cannot) do another thing, but . . .

1. *also* goes between the special verb 'can' and the other verb:
> I can cook; I can *also* sew.
2. *too/as well* go at the end of a sentence:
> I can play the guitar; I can play the piano *too*.
3. *either* goes at the end of a negative sentence:
> She can't sing; she can't dance *either*.

Look at the police documents again. You can see that Bert is 58 years old, and Joe is 60. We can compare them like this:

> Joe is older than his brother.
> Bert is younger than his brother.

This is called the comparative.

Comparatives

The comparative is used when describing or comparing two people, two things, or two groups of people or things. It can be formed in two ways:

1. The adjective + *er* on the end, followed by *than*. Use this form in short words of only one or two sounds (syllables), so long as they don't end in –ly or –ful:

> old → older than
> dark → darker than
> clever → cleverer than
> gentle → gentler than

Remember . . . Words with one vowel and one consonant change by doubling the consonant and adding –*er*, like this:

> Bert is fat.   Joe is fat*ter* than Bert.
> Bert has a big head.   Joe has a big*ger* head than Bert.

Words ending in a consonant + y change to –*ier*:

> Joe is ugly, but Bert is ugl*ier* than Joe.

2. The second comparative form: *more/less* + adjective or adverb + *than*. Use this with long words of three or more sounds (syllables), and with words ending in –ly, –ful.

> important, incredible, dangerous
> slowly, awful, quickly

> Joe is a *more* dangerous criminal *than* Bert.
> Bert is a *less* dangerous criminal *than* Joe.
> Joe can run *more* quickly *than* his brother.

Irregular forms:

> good → better than
> bad → worse than
> little → less than
> far → farther than

Look at the picture below and compare the answers of the two girls. They both want a job as a secretary; a man is interviewing them.

Man	Fiona Smythe	Mandy Jones
What's your name?	Fiona Smythe.	Mandy.
How old are you?	I'm 24.	I'm 17.
Where do you live?	I live at 2 Bath Road.	I live in Clapham.
How far is that from here?	It's only half a mile away.	It's about ten miles away.
Are you married?	No, I'm single.	No, but I'm engaged.
Can you type?	Yes I can.	No I can't.
How many other languages can you speak?	I can speak French, German and Italian.	I can speak a bit of (= a little) Welsh.
Can you drive?	Yes I can.	Not very well.
What else can you do?	I can take notes in shorthand and use a photocopier.	I can make coffee and answer the phone.
What time do you usually get up?	At about half past six (6.30).	At a quarter to nine (8.45).
Do you want to ask me any questions?	Yes please. How much overtime (= extra time) can I do?	Can I have Wednesday afternoon off (= free from work)?

EXERCISE 15

1) What day is it?
2) What time is it in each picture?
3) How old is Mandy?
4) Where does Fiona live?
5) Does Mandy know shorthand?
6) Does Mandy live close to the office?
7) Are the girls married?
8) Can Fiona drive?
9) Can Mandy answer the phone?

EXERCISE 16

Copy and complete:
1) Mandy is younger ___ ___ .
2) Mandy lives farther away ___ ___ .
3) Fiona knows more foreign languages ___ ___ .
4) ___ gets up earlier ___ ___ .
5) ___ ___ older ___ ___ .
6) ___ gets up later than ___ .
7) ___ lives closer to the office ___ ___ .
8) Fiona drives better ___ ___ .
9) ___ drives worse than ___ .
10) Mandy speaks fewer languages ___ ___ .
11) Fiona can speak German. She can ___ ___ and ___ too.
12) Mandy can't speak German. She can't ___ ___ or ___ either.
13) Mandy can make coffee; she can ___ ___ ___ too.
14) Mandy can't take notes in shorthand; she can't ___ ___ ___ either.
15) Which of the two girls gives better answers?

EXERCISE 17   Now make sentences like this:
Mandy is lazier than Fiona because *she gets up later* in the morning.
1) Fiona looks smarter than Mandy because . . . . better dressed.
2) Fiona is cleverer than Mandy because . . . . languages.
3) Fiona is more interested in the job because . . . . work.
4) Mandy knows less about office work because . . . . shorthand.

EXERCISE 18   Write sentences comparing the two girls, using *more, less, fewer*.
For example:

Mandy	Fiona
has 12 dresses	15 dresses *Mandy has fewer dresses than Fiona.*
1) has 3 cats	1 cat
2) has 6 coats	2 coats
3) weighs 8 stone or 51 kg	9½ stone or 60 kg
4) has short hair	long hair
5) has 2 sisters	3 sisters
6) is 158 centimetres tall	166 centimetres tall
7) has £400 in the bank	£50 in the bank
8) has 30 records	12 records

Future with *going to*

This is formed by the present continuous tense of the verb *go* + *to* + the present simple:

I am going	to	work	tomorrow
are you going	to	work	tomorrow?

The form is used to indicate
1. an *intention* in the future:
Tom is going to buy a car next week.
We're going to invite Mary to the party tomorrow.

2. an *opinion* about the future:
It isn't going to rain.
He is going to be ill soon.

Use *in* with a period of time:
They are going to start work *in a few minutes.*
We are going to move house *in three months' time.*
He's going to buy it *in a fortnight* (= two weeks).
It's going to rain *in a moment* (= almost immediately).

Look at the picture series below and note the prepositions in *italic* print.

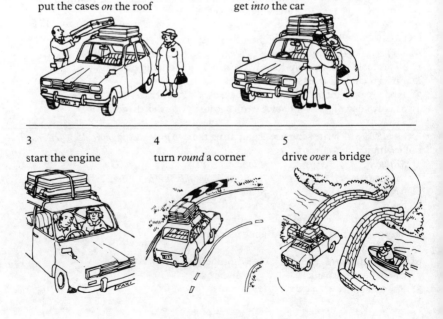

1
put the cases *on* the roof

2
get *into* the car

3
start the engine

4
turn *round* a corner

5
drive *over* a bridge

6
go *through* a tunnel

7
walk *across* the road

8
slow down *behind* a lorry

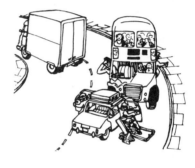

9
overtake the lorry and crash *into* a bus

10
fall *off* the roof

EXERCISE 19

Write down what is going to happen in each picture. For example:

1) *The taxi-driver is going to put the cases on the roof.*
2) The old lady . . .
3) The driver . . .
4) He's . . .
5) He's . . .
6) He's . . .
7) Some people . . .
8) The car . . .
9) It's . . .
10) The cases . . .

EXERCISE 20

Extra questions:

1) What is the boat in No. 5 going to do?   (go under)
2) What is the driver in No. 7 going to do?   (slow down)
3) What is the bus-driver in No. 9 going to do?   (shout at)
4) What is the lady in No. 10 going to do?   (get out of)

Look at this picture. Bert, the burglar, is entering someone's flat. He is going to steal some jewels and a fur coat. He's going to take some money out of her handbag and he's also going to take the painting off the wall.

EXERCISE 21

Now answer the questions below, filling in the blank spaces.

1) Where are the jewels? *They are in* __ __ .
2) Where is the fur coat? *It is* __ __ *wardrobe.*
3) Where is the handbag? *It's* __ __ __ .
4) Where is the painting? *It's on* __ __ .
5) Is the wardrobe in front of Bert or behind him? *It's* __ __ __ __ .
6) Where is the lady standing? *She's* __ __ __ __ .
7) Where is the policeman, inside the room or outside? *He is* __ __ __ .
8) What is Bert going to do with his gloves? *He is* __ __ *put them on.*
9) What is the lady going to do? *She is* __ __ *hit Bert.*
10) What's the clock going to do in two minutes' time? *It's* __ __ *strike.*
11) What is the policeman going to do? *He's* __ __ *arrest Bert.*
12) Where's the policeman going to take him? *He's* __ __ __
__ __ *prison.*
13) Does Bert know what is going to happen to him? __ __ __ .
14) What does he think he is going to do? *He thinks he's* __ __ __ __ .

EXERCISE 22

The ten sentences below are *untrue* – change then into *true* statements.

EXAMPLE: The handbag is in the wardrobe. (*untrue*)
The handbag is on the table. (*true*)

1) The jewels are under the drawer.
2) Bert is going to take his gloves off.
3) The lady is standing in front of the door.
4) The clock is going to strike in twenty minutes.
5) Bert is going to put on a fur coat.
6) Bert is going to hang a picture on the wall.
7) Bert is going to arrest the policeman.
8) The lady is going to hit him with her handbag.
9) Bert is going to leave the jewels in the drawer.
10) Bert is going to spend two years at the seaside.

Sandra:	Tell me, am I going to have a happy future?
Fortune Teller:	I can't see very much yet. Wait a moment.
Sandra:	Am I going to meet anyone?
Fortune Teller:	Yes you are. I can see a tall, dark man. He's going to take you out in his sports-car.
Sandra:	When am I going to meet him?
Fortune Teller:	In about two years' time. Here is something else. You're going to take an exam.
Sandra:	That's right. Am I going to pass?
Fortune Teller:	I can see a dark cloud. I'm sorry dear, that means you're going to fail. Oh no!
Sandra:	What's the matter? What else is going to happen?
Fortune Teller:	You're going to break a mirror and a lot of unlucky things are going to follow.
Sandra:	What kind of things?
Fortune Teller:	I'm afraid you're going to have a lot of accidents. You're going to fall off a horse and then you're going to fall into a lake; you're even going to fall out of bed.

Sandra:	Fall out of bed? What about the man in the sports-car – can you still see him?
Fortune Teller:	Yes I can. He's coming out of church, beside a girl in a white dress. They are going to get into a car. It says 'Just Married'. The girl isn't you, I'm afraid.
Sandra:	How much are you going to charge me for telling me all this?
Fortune Teller:	Only 75p, dear.
Sandra:	Wait a moment! I can see someone in the crystal ball now.
Fortune Teller:	Oh yes? What can you see?
Sandra:	A very angry girl, and she says she isn't going to pay you!

Two hours later Sandra is telling her mother about this visit – write down what you think she says:

> The fortune-teller thinks I'm going to have a lot of bad luck. I'm going . . .

EXERCISE 23

Now answer questions 1–4, and in questions 5–10 say which of the answers given is the correct one.

1) What kind of man is Sandra going to meet?
2) Is she going to go out in his sports-car?
3) Is she going to marry the man?
4) What is going to happen to Sandra after she breaks the mirror?

5) Sandra is going to have a lot of
—nice surprises.
—happiness.
—accidents.

6) Sandra is going to meet a tall dark man
—in a moment.
—after a long time.

7) Sandra isn't going to
—give the fortune-teller any money.
—fall off a horse.
—fail her exams.

8) The tall, dark man is going to marry
—Sandra.
—another girl.
—the fortune-teller.

9) Sandra is going to
—drive into a lake.
—go to church.
—have a lot of bad luck.

10) After her visit to the fortune-teller she is
—angry.
—afraid.
—pleased.

The past tenses

Introduction

Verbs in English have three basic forms:

1	2	3
simple present	simple past	past participle
walk	walked	walked

The past of *regular* verbs like 'walk' is formed by adding –*ed* to the present tense. Notice how some regular verbs (such as 'stop', 'study') add an extra letter or change their spelling in the same way as in the present tenses (see page 9).

1	2	3
stop	stop*ped*	stop*ped*
study	stud*ied*	stud*ied*

Many verbs are *irregular* (see page 114 for a complete list). Their past tenses are formed by:

a) a different word

1	2	3
buy	bought	bought
sell	sold	sold

b) a different word for each tense

1	2	3
go	went	gone
give	gave	given

c) the same word as the present

1	2	3
put	put	put
cut	cut	cut

The simple past

To form this tense, add *-ed* to the simple present tense.

Simple present   Simple past

| I, you, he etc
walk | +-ed → | I, you, he etc
walked |

The word *walked* is the past participle of the verb. Some verbs have irregular past participles that are not formed as above, and which must be learned as you meet them. A list of irregular verbs is given on page 114. Three common examples are:

> I buy→I bought
> I go→I went
> I put →I put

In questions and negatives (*not/n't*), use *did* or *didn't* with the simple present:
> Did you stop?
> I didn't go.

This tense tells us what is past and finished. It is also used for telling stories. When do you use it? . . .

1. With words of time (referring to a completed action).

| I met Jill
I didn't meet Jill | yesterday
in 1976
last year
on Saturday
at 6pm. |

2. The *idea* of time
> I talked to Jill at the party. (= on Saturday night)
> I didn't talk to Jill after lunch. (= in the afternoon)

3. A period of time *in the past*
> Jill worked in an office for three years, 1975–1978. She doesn't work there now.

4. With *ago* (this comes after a word of time)
> It's Thursday *now*.   I met Jill last Monday.
>   (= I met Jill three days *ago*).

Notice that in all examples there is an exact time mentioned – we know when the event happened.

Sandra is looking at her diary – it is Sunday morning. Her boyfriend Mick is talking to her.

'I didn't see you last week, Sandra. How did you spend your time?'

EXERCISE 24

Write down and complete Sandra's replies:
On Monday I went shopping and bought a dress and a hat.
1) On Tuesday I went to the cinema and saw a ___ .
2) On Wednesday I went to a disco and met ___ .
3) On Thursday I went to the hairdresser's and read a ___ .
4) On Friday I went to a restaurant and ate some ___ .
5) On Saturday I stayed at home and listened to a ___ .

EXERCISE 25

Now answer these questions – turn to page 114 for the verb forms.
1) What did Sandra do (a) yesterday, (b) on Tuesday, (c) three days ago?
2) How much money did she spend (a) in the shop, (b) at the cinema, (c) in the restaurant?
3) What did she (a) eat, and (b) drink in the restaurant?
4) Did she go to the cinema on Tuesday? *Yes she did.*
   a) Did she meet David on Tuesday? ___ ___ *didn't.*
   b) Did she go to a disco last night? ___ ___ ___ .
   c) Did she go to a restaurant two days ago? ___ ___ ___ . .

EXERCISE 26

Now make questions for Sandra's replies. For example:

I went to the cinema. = What did you do on Tuesday?

1) *I went to a restaurant.*	What did ___ ___ ___ ___ ?
2) *I spent £8.50.*	How much did ___ ___ ___ ___ ___ ?
3) *I met David.*	Who did ___ ___ ___ ___ ___ ?
4) *I read a magazine.*	What did ___ ___ ___ ___ ___ ?
5) *It cost £15.*	How much did ___ ___ ___ ?
6) *I stayed at home.*	What did ___ ___ ___ ?
7) *I met him four days ago.*	When did ___ ___ ___ ?
8) *I went to the cinema.*	Where did ___ ___ ___ ___ ?

Remember . . . 'Time' words go at the beginning or end of the sentence, *not in the middle.* For example: 'In 1976 I went to Paris' *or* 'I went to Paris in 1976'.

Prepositions of time

at + exact time	Christmas. Easter. 6 o'clock.
in + period of time	May. Summer. 1960. The 20th century.
on + a day or date	Monday. My birthday. 2nd June.
for + length of time	I worked for two hours and twenty minutes.

Two special verbs which do *not* have 'did' in the past form:

a) **I am:**

I am he/she/it is there is	I was *etc*	I wasn't *etc*	was I? *etc*
you are we are they are there are	you were *etc*	you weren't *etc*	were you? *etc*

b) **I can:**

I can	I could	I couldn't	could I?

Have and **do** These are normal verbs; check p. 31 for the names of the three basic forms numbered 1, 2, 3.

1	2	3
have	had	had
do	did	done

> I had an icecream yesterday.
> Did you have an icecream?
> I didn't have an icecream yesterday.
> I did the shopping on Saturday.
> Did you do the shopping?
> I didn't do the shopping on Saturday.

Superlatives

The comparative is used when describing or comparing two people or things (see page 23). The superlative is used when describing or comparing three or more people or things. It is formed by putting *the* before the adjective, which has *–est* added on, or by putting *the most* before the unchanged adjective.

> Mount Everest is *the* high*est* mountain in the world.
> Rolls Royces are *the most* expensive cars in Britain.

Look again at page 23 and note the same spelling changes for the superlative as for the comparative.

> big →big*ger*→big*gest*
> ugly→ugl*ier*→ugl*iest*

Note: better→the best   worse→the worst
           more→the most   less →the least

Greta, Hans and Maria spent their holidays in England last summer. Compare their different impressions and answer the questions on the next page.

Greta:

I had a pleasant time in London and stayed with an English family for five weeks. It didn't cost me much and I bought some very cheap clothes and souvenirs in the street markets. I often travelled by boat on the River Thames. I found it was the best way to see London. I particularly like Kew Gardens. It's the most beautiful and the cheapest park in the world; it cost me only 10p to go in! I also went to Greenwich, and to Hampton Court with its famous maze and kitchens. Henry VIII lived there and built the oldest tennis court in existence. There wasn't any fog in London but it was rather cloudy and I always wore a coat.

Hans:

I had a terrible time and stayed at the worst hotel in London. I stayed for only ten days and then left. The centre of the city was crowded and noisy and I couldn't find an English restaurant. I always travelled on the underground and often got lost. On my first afternoon in London, someone stole my wallet. I told a policeman but he couldn't understand my English. Then I couldn't get any more money because the banks close at 3.30. There was another thing I didn't like: the pubs closed at 10.30 and the buses stopped running at about 11 o'clock, so I always went to bed very early. The weather was awful – it rained every day.

Maria:

I had a wonderful holiday and travelled by car to the West of England and North Wales. I spent the best three weeks of my life. I saw three magnificent cathedrals at Gloucester, Wells and Salisbury – perhaps Gloucester is the finest cathedral in Europe. The food in the country is better than in London; the most delicious things I had were Double Gloucester cheese and West Country cider. I went up Snowdon by train and came down on foot. It's the highest mountain in England and Wales. The castles in Wales are really spectacular and the scenery is beautiful. I took a lot of photos because it was very sunny every day.

EXERCISE 27

1) Which visitor had a) the most enjoyable holiday?
                   b) the least enjoyable holiday?
                   c) the best weather?
                   d) the worst weather?
                   e) the longest time in Britain?
                   f) the shortest time in Britain?
2) What did Greta say was the best way to see London?
3) How did Hans and Maria travel?
4) What did Greta like about Kew Gardens?
5) Where is the oldest tennis court in the world?
6) Why did Hans dislike his hotel?
7) What did Maria think about Gloucester Cathedral?
8) What food did Maria enjoy most?
9) What is the highest mountain in England and Wales?
10) Which of the three visitors was the luckiest and which of the three was the unluckiest?
11) What did Greta buy?
12) Where did she stay?
13) Where did Henry VIII live?
14) What did Maria admire in Wales?
15) What did she do with her camera?

Complete these sentences:
16) Greta liked Kew Gardens because . . . .
17) The policeman didn't help Hans because . . . .
18) Hans couldn't change his money because . . . .
19) Hans went to bed early because . . . .
20) Hans only stayed in London for 10 days because . . . .

EXERCISE 28

Write down and complete this story. Change the verbs in brackets to the past tense and fill the empty spaces with a preposition.

Three men (go) to have lunch in a cafe ___ one o'clock ___ Saturday. They (aren't) very hungry and (don't have) much to eat. Tom and Jerry (have) sandwiches. Fred (want) to have fish and chips but there (isn't) any and the waiter (give) him a meat pie instead. After lunch they (drink) some coffee and (smoke) cigarettes ___ a few minutes. ___ about five past two the waiter (bring) them the bill. It (is) exactly £3.
'(Do you enjoy) your meal?' he (ask).
'Yes I (do)' (reply) Fred 'but it (is) an expensive pie.'
Each man (give) the waiter £1 and then (put) on their coats. A moment later the waiter (come) back and (say):
'I'm very sorry, I (make) a mistake just now – your bill (come) to only £2.50 and not £3.
So he (put) 50p back on the table. The men (think) ___ a few moments because

they (can't) divide 50 between three people. Eventually they (take) 10p each and (leave) the waiter 20p as a tip because he (is) very honest.
They (go) out of the cafe and then Fred suddenly (look) worried.

'How much (do you pay) Tom?'
'First I (pay) £1; then the waiter (give) me back 10p. So the meal (cost) me 90p.'
'Well, Jerry (pay) 90p and I did too. That makes £2.70.'
'That's right.'
'How much (do we leave) for the waiter?'
'20p.'
'That makes £2.90. I (think) we (give) the waiter £3. Where's the other 10p?'

The past tense denoting *habit*

This is formed by adding the simple present tense to *used to*, the negative of which is *never used to* or *used not to*. Use this tense to show a change in habit or circumstance:

> I *used to* smoke 20 cigarettes a day. (Now I smoke five.)
> My parents *used to* live in Scotland. (Now they live in London.)
> Jean *never used to/used not to* eat much. (Now she eats a lot.)

Here are two pictures of the same man. Picture 1 shows Mr Burns 30 years ago; picture 2 shows Mr Burns now.

EXERCISE 29

Form sentences like this:
1) Mr Burns used to have long hair *but now he has short hair*.
2) He used to ride a bike *but now* ___ ___ ___ ___ .
3) He used to have a beard *but* ___ ___ ___ ___ ___ .
4) He used to wear a pair of old jeans ___ ___ ___ ___ ___ ___ .
5) He used to be poor ___ ___ ___ ___ ___ .
6) ___ ___ ___ ___ ___ but now he is married.
7) He used not to work ___ ___ ___ ___ a businessman.
8) ___ ___ ___ ___ ___ but now he is fat.
9) He never used to smoke but ___ ___ ___ ___ .
10) ___ ___ ___ ___ books but now he just reads the newspaper.

The present perfect

To form this tense, take *have* or *has* and add to it the past participle:

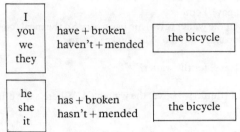

| I you we they | have + broken haven't + mended | the bicycle |

| he she it | has + broken hasn't + mended | the bicycle |

Question form:

Have I broken the bicycle?
Haven't you mended the bicycle?
Has she broken the bicycle?
Hasn't he mended the bicycle?

Use these short forms in conversation:

I have = I've   he has = he's
you have = you've   she has = she's
we have = we've   it has = it's
they have = they've   John has = John's

When do you use the present perfect tense?
Use it to record events in the past when there is no mention of exact time, or idea of when something happened:

John has sold his car.   I have bought an umbrella.

EXERCISE 30
Look at these pictures and write down *what has happened*

pass   win   score a goal   buy   find

1) Why is Jack smiling?
   a) He has (he's) passed his exam.
   b)
   c)
   d)
   e)

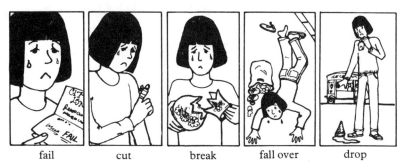

| fail | cut | break | fall over | drop |

2) Why is Judy crying?
   f) She has (she's) failed her exam.
   g)
   h)
   i)
   j)

Notice how the present perfect tense is used with these phrases:
   I have drunk four cups of coffee   — today
                                        — this week
                                        — this month
   I have visited eight countries   — this year
                                        — in my life.

EXERCISE 31

Mrs Burns and Sandra found their living-room like this when
they got up this morning   Now it is like this

Find one word from the list below and say what they have done to:

1) the dishes? *They have washed up the dishes.*
2) the carpets?
3) the ashtrays?
4) the newspapers?
5) the silver?
6) the shelves?
7) the windows?
8) the books?
close, polish, sweep, put away, fold up, empty, dust, washed up.

EXERCISE 32

Write out these questions and fill in the blank with a verb from the list that follows: *spent, eaten, drunk, used, seen, read, made, written.* (Some verbs may be used more than once.) For example, the first answer would be *How many cups of coffee have you drunk this week?*

1) How many cups of coffee have you ___ this week?
2) How many films have you ___ this week?
3) How many books have you ___ this week?
4) How many cakes have you ___ this week?
5) How many letters have you ___ this week?
6) How many phone calls have you ___ this week?
7) How much sugar have you ___ this week?
8) How much money have you ___ this week?
9) How much petrol have you ___ this week?
10) How much coca-cola have you ___ this week?

Now answer these same questions yourself. For example, your reply to the first one could be:
I've drunk two cups of coffee. Or: *I haven't drunk any.*

Words often used with the present perfect tense

1. *already/yet*

Look at these sentences:

> John has finished his lunch *already*. (positive = he's finished eating it)
> I haven't finished my lunch *yet*. (negative = I'm still eating it)
> Have you finished your lunch *yet*? (= are you still eating it?)
> Have you finished your lunch *already*? (= I'm surprised, you were very quick)

EXERCISE 33

Write down pairs of sentences like this:

> Derek can drive his father's car; he has passed his driving-test already.
> Sandra can't drive it; she hasn't passed her test yet.

1) Derek doesn't want to read the newspaper; *he's read it already.*
   Sandra wants ___ ___ ___ ___ ; ___ ___ ___ ___ ___ ___ .
2) Derek doesn't want to see the Tower of London; ___ ___ ___ ___ .
   Sandra wants to ___ ___ ___ ___ ; ___ ___ ___ ___ .
3) Derek doesn't need any skiing lessons. He's had ___ ___ .
   Sandra needs ___ ___ ; ___ ___ ___ ___ ___ .
4) Derek doesn't want any coffee; ___ ___ ___ ___ .
   Sandra wants ___ ___ ; ___ ___ ___ ___ ___ .

2. *just/recently/lately*

Use the present perfect tense with *just* to express a recently completed action, where 'just' means 'very recently'. Put it between the auxiliary (have/has) and the main verb:

It's 8 o'clock in the morning. Sandra is in bed and the alarm clock is ringing. She has *just* woken up.

In general, *recently* and *lately* go *after* the verb, at the end of the clause or sentence:

> Tom has spent a lot of money *recently*.

3. *ever*

Used in the examples below, 'ever' means 'in your life' or 'at any time in the past':

> Have you *ever* seen a ghost?
> Have you *ever* eaten paella?

If the answer to a question with the word 'ever' in it is negative, you need to use the word '*never*' in your reply; (*never* is the abbreviation that you must always use for *not ever*). For example, if you wanted to say 'no' to the two questions above, you would answer

> No, I have *never* seen a ghost.
> No, I have *never* eaten paella.

Special note

The present perfect forms of *I am, we are, you are, they are, there are* are:

I we you they there	have been

(The above examples can be abbreviated to I've been, we've been, etc.)

The present perfect forms of *he is, she is, it is, there is* are:

he she it there	has been etc

(These examples can be abbreviated to he's been, she's been, etc.)

> In my life, I *have been* a student, a soldier and a farmer; now I'm a businessman.
> There *have been* a lot of wars in this country.

42

She *has been* ill, but she's better now.
It *has been* a good summer; *there's been* a lot of sun.

Important: *Have been to = Have visited*
Have you ever been abroad? (= Have you ever visited any other countries?)
Yes I have.   I've been to Japan once. (One time)
                 I've been to India twice. (Two times)
                 I've been to America five times.

The present perfect continuous tense

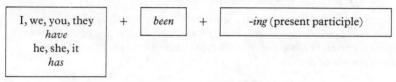

Read the sentence below, and the two examples showing this tense.
         Mr Burns lit a cigar at eight o'clock. It's 8.10 now and he's still smoking it.
         He *has been smoking* a cigar *since* eight o'clock.
         or . . . He *has been smoking* a cigar *for* ten minutes.
This tense is generally used to describe an action that began in the past and is still happening now. Use it with verbs that continue over a period of time: 'wait', 'sleep', 'study', 'read', 'live', 'eat'.

EXERCISE 34
Make sentences like the one below, using the verbs shown in *italics*.

EXAMPLE: Tom went to sleep at 10pm. It's 3am now and he's snoring.
         Sleep — He has been sleeping since ten o'clock.
         — He has been sleeping for five hours.
1) Mr and Mrs Burns bought their house six years ago. They are still living there now.
   Live — They . . .
2) I started learning English two months ago. I'm still learning it.
   Learn — I . . .
3) Jack bought a sports car nine months ago. He's still driving it.
   Drive — He . . .
4) Susan went to the bus-stop at 10.15. It's 10.55 now and the bus still hasn't come.
   Wait — She . . .
5) Sid began lunch at 1 o'clock. It's 1.45 now and he's just started his pudding.
   Eat — He . . .
6) Tony bought a novel from a bookshop on Monday. It's Saturday now and he has reached page 400.
   Read — He . . .

EXERCISE 35

What do you think has been happening in these situations?
EXAMPLE: Everything outside is white. = *It has been snowing.*
1) The dog is panting. =
2) Mick is on the beach. He's wet. =
3) Ted is putting away his lawnmower. The grass is short. =
4) The cat looks happy. There is a fish-bone on the floor. =
5) Tommy has a black eye. =
6) George is angry. He's standing at a bus stop. =

Read this television interview and answer the questions below:

Elsie Frost has just reached the age of 90; the producer of the programme 'My life and memories' has invited her to the studio tonight.

Interviewer: Welcome to 'My life and memories'. First I want to begin by wishing you a happy birthday.
Elsie: Thank you very much, dear.
Interviewer: How long have you been living in London, Elsie?
Elsie: All my life. And I've loved every minute of it.
Interviewer: Have you ever been abroad?
Elsie: Well, I used to go on day-trips to Calais. That was when my husband was still alive.
Interviewer: I believe you have been married more than once.
Elsie: Yes, I've been married twice and engaged six times.
Interviewer: Has London changed much since you were a little girl?
Elsie: Good Lord yes! There used not to be all those ugly high buildings, noisy supermarkets and horrible snack-bars. People used to have more time for a laugh and a chat and they used to enjoy their food too. On the other hand, most people are friendlier now than they used to be; they don't lose their tempers and shout so much.
Interviewer: That's interesting! Tell me, you used to be an actress, didn't you?
Elsie: Used to be? I still am. I haven't retired yet. I've just started in a new play.
Interviewer: Really! How long have you been acting?
Elsie: For the last fifty years. I've also been a singer and a dancer.
Interviewer: Are audiences different from what they used to be?
Elsie: Oh yes, they used to be much ruder than they are now. They used to shout and boo. I remember once forty years ago they threw tomatoes at the actors. But now they have become very polite and the theatre has become less exciting.
Interviewer: Have you done everything that you wanted to in your life?
Elsie: No, I haven't. I've never been to Hollywood.
Interviewer: Well, good luck. I hope you have enjoyed coming here tonight.

EXERCISE 36

1) Find a word in the interview with the same meaning as:
   a) to like   *b*) journeys   *c*) to another country   *d*) get angry
   e) conversation   *f*) unattractive   *g*) awful   *h*) well-mannered
2) How old is Elsie?
3) Why is she appearing on TV tonight?
4) How many husbands has she had?
5) Where used she to live when she was a little girl?
6) What does she dislike about modern life?
7) In what way does Elsie think life is better today than it used to be?
8) How used audiences to behave when they disliked a play?
9) When did Elsie start acting?
10) Write down:
   a) one thing Elsie used to be
   b) an unpleasant memory of something in the theatre
   c) something she wants to do

The past continuous tense

I, he, she, it	*was*	(*wasn't*)		-*ing* (present participle)
you, we, they	*were*	(*weren't*)	+	

I was crossing the road.
They weren't listening.

How to use it:
Use this tense for a *continuous* action that began *before* the time mentioned.

Mr Thompson's plane took off from Rome at 6pm. It landed in London at 8pm. At 7pm *he was sitting* in the plane.

He didn't sit down at seven o'clock. He sat down at six o'clock.

What else was happening on the plane at 7pm?

The pilot was flying the plane.
The air-hostesses were serving a snack.
Several passengers were sleeping.

Look at this picture and answer the questions in the past continuous tense.

EXERCISE 37

A friend of Derek's came to the Burns' house last night. When he knocked on the door, nobody heard him. Why not?

1) What was Mrs Burns doing?
2) Did she hear a knock on the door?
3) Was she speaking to her husband?
4) What was her husband doing?
5) What was he holding in his hand?
6) Was he making much noise?
7) What was Grandpa watching?
8) What were Derek and Sandra listening to?
9) What was the weather like outside?
10) What was Derek's friend carrying?
11) Were any cars going by outside?
12) What was going by?
13) Why do you think nobody heard Derek's friend?

Reflexive pronouns

Here are the reflexive pronouns:

myself	ourselves
yourself	yourselves
himself, herself, itself	themselves

Sheila is looking at Mark.

Sheila is looking at *herself* in the mirror.

When two or more people share an action, use *each other*:
Sheila and Mark are looking at *each other*.

Write down the sentences in Exercise 38 and fill the empty spaces with a reflexive pronoun or 'each other'.
Note that 'while' = 'when' and is usually used with a continuous verb form.

EXERCISE 38

1) Bill cut ____ while he was shaving.
2) The children enjoyed ____ while they were staying in the country.
3) I cut ____ while I was peeling the potatoes.
4) We hurt ____ while we were playing football.
5) They shook hands with ____ ____ when they met.
6) They danced with ____ ____ while the band was playing.
7) The soldier shot ____ while he was cleaning his gun.
8) The students whispered to ____ ____ while the teacher was writing on the blackboard.

Special note: Many verbs use *get* + past participle instead of the reflexive form: Common examples of these are:

get engaged	get married	get divorced
get ready	get dressed	get undressed
get lost	get broken	get torn

Past perfect

Had + past participle
Use this form when you mention *two actions* in the past and you want to show *one* action *happened before* the other.
Compare these sentences:

> Jim came to my house yesterday; he *broke* his arm.
> = he broke his arm *while* he was in my house.
> Jim came to my house yesterday; he *had broken* his arm.
> = he broke his arm *before* he came to my house.

Use *had/hadn't* with all pronouns: I had . . ., you hadn't . . .
In conversation you can use: I'd/you'd/he'd/we'd/they'd (not).
The past perfect tense is very often used with these words:

> after
> when
> as soon as (= immediately after)

Join the pairs of sentences in Exercise 39 like this:

> John ate three cream cakes. *Then* he felt sick.
> = *After* John had eaten three cream cakes, he felt sick.
> He finished his meal. *Then* straightaway he left the restaurant.
> = *As soon* as he had finished his meal, he left the restaurant.

EXERCISE 39

1) They shook hands. Then they sat down.
   After . . .
2) The cowboy entered the bar. He immediately shot the barman.
   As soon as . . .
3) Fred ate some shepherd's pie. Then he had some rice pudding.
   When . . .
4) He drank a glass of brandy. He choked.
   As soon as . . .
5) The thief robbed a bank, broke into a house and stole a car. Then the police arrested him.
   After . . .
6) Dick didn't do any work. His boss sacked him.
   Dick's boss sacked him because . . .
7) Bob forgot Sue's name. He didn't ask her to dance with him.
   Bob didn't ask Sue to dance with him because . . .
8) Mike filled his car with petrol. He drove off.
   When . . .
9) The waiter opened a bottle of champagne. He poured out a drink.
   As soon as . . .
10) He switched off the light. He went to bed.
    After . . .

Reported (or *indirect*) Speech

When you record the *exact words* a person uses in English, it is called *direct* speech and it must be enclosed by inverted commas ('...'). The words may be from conversation:

> He said, 'I love Susan'.
> He said, 'I'll ring you back'.

or a quotation from a book or speech:

> Dr Johnson said, 'When a man is tired of London, he is tired of life'.

However, each of these remarks can be reported *indirectly*, so that the speaker's exact words are not given but the meaning is exactly retained. In this case don't use inverted commas:

> He said (that) he loved Susan.
> He said (that) he would ring me back.
> Dr Johnson said that when a man is tired of London, he is tired of life. (Note that when the truth of a quotation is unquestioned, it remains in the present.)

Reported speech most commonly occurs after a verb in the past tense, and there are certain changes in the sentence:

1. The personal pronoun
   I, we, our usually change to *he, they, their*
   you usually changes to *me* or *him/them*
2. The word 'that' should be used after the introducing verb but is sometimes omitted, particularly in conversation.
3. Whichever tense of a verb is used in direct speech must be changed into the corresponding past tense (literally the next tense back) in reported speech. Note the table below and the following examples.

I go	He said (that) he went.
I went/have gone	He said (that) he had gone.
I am going	He said (that) he was going.
I'll go	He said (that) he would go.
I was going I've been going	He said (that) he had been going.
I can go	He said (that) he could go.
I may go	He said (that) he might go.
I must go	He said (that) he had to go.

She said, 'I *am going* to watch a film'.
She said (that) she *was going* to watch a film.
He said, 'I *was running* faster than my brother'.
He said (that) he *had been running* faster than his brother.

Note that with some of the special verbs – 'ought to', 'should', 'might' – there is no change in reported speech.
Some other necessary changes, mostly relating to time, are shown below:

today	that day
yesterday	the day before (the previous day)
tomorrow	the day after (the following day)
this/these	that/those
here	there
two days ago	two days before
now	at that time

For example:

> She said, 'I'll see you tomorrow'.
> She said (that) she would see me the following day.
> He said, 'I left my hat here'.
> He said (that) he had left his hat there.

4. The verb *tell/told* (= inform) is a very common introducing word. It must be followed by a noun or pronoun *without* 'to'. Other verbs like this are *inform, warn* and *advise*:

> He told *us* (that) he was hungry./I'll tell David we're waiting.

Verbs like *say, complain, suggest* must have 'to' before a noun or pronoun:

> He said that the meat was bad./He complained *to* the manager that the meat was bad.

EXERCISE 40

Using the model to help you, change the following remarks into reported speech (change *you* to *I*). For example:

> 'I'm going to a party tomorrow.' *He told me he was going to a party on the following day.*

1) 'I want some beer.'
2) 'I don't understand this problem.'
3) 'I broke these plates yesterday.'
4) 'You didn't phone me last week.'
5) 'We have won the match.'
6) 'I haven't had any breakfast.'
7) 'You're going to be late.'
8) 'Sam is buying a car today.'
9) 'I was going to cross the road when I saw a sports car coming.'
10) 'I've been studying English for four months.'
11) 'You can't drive.'
12) 'Tom will be late if he doesn't hurry.'
13) 'I won't forget to post your letter.'
14) 'I must wait here for Sally.'
15) 'You should change your job.'

Indirect questions

who/what/when/where/how old, etc may be used after a 'question' verb such as *ask, inquire, know, wonder.*

Make the same changes as for reported speech and remember to change the order of words, as in these examples:

'How old *are you?*'   I'll ask him how old *he is.*
'When *did you learn* French?'   I asked him when *he learnt* French.
'Where *does* Kay *live?*'   I wonder where Kay *lives.*

Requesting information

ask + if/whether (also *wonder/want to know*):

'Are you going to the party'   He asked me *if* I was going to the party.
'Do you want any more soup?'   The waiter asked *whether* they wanted more soup.

Note that *ask + to* has a different meaning. It introduces a polite command:

The teacher *asked* us *to* make less noise.

Points to remember

a) Don't use a question mark in indirect questions.
b) The subject goes before the verb.
c) The tense of the verb changes as in the models on reported speech.

Special note

The infinitive form is often used in indirect questions when the subject of the introducing verb is the same as in the question:

I don't know where I will park my car.
= I don't know *where to park* my car.
She doesn't know who she should invite.
= She doesn't know *whom to invite.*

EXERCISE 41

Look at this situation. Tony has been invited to play tennis tomorrow. He has never played tennis in his life before. Make as many sentences as you can beginning *Tony doesn't know . . .* choosing a question word from list A and a phrase from list B. For example: Tony doesn't know *how to score.*

A	B
where	to do
what	to stand
when	to play with
who	to score
how	to wear
whether	to hold the racquet
how many	to stand near the net
	to hit the ball
	balls to play with

Future tenses

Simple future

There are several ways of expressing the future in English, one of which is by using the simple future tense. This itself can be formed either by *will* + the simple present or by *shall* + the simple present. The *will* form is more correctly used when the speaker wants to express determination or promise, whereas the *shall* form suggests only that something is going to happen (for example) in the future. But because both forms are so often shortened and then appear to be identical – see below – you need not worry too much about which to use.

I, he, she, it we, you, they	will/won't	help

I, we	shall/shan't	help

Note how the negative (I *will not* help, I *shall not* help) may be shortened (I *won't* help, I *shan't* help).

In conversation, always use these short forms in positive sentences: I'll, he'll, she'll, it'll, we'll, you'll, they'll.

A simple rule to remember is that you may use 'shall' *or* 'will' after 'I' and 'we', but stick to using 'will' after the other pronouns. Use the simple future form for making *definite* statements about the future:

> *I'll see* you tomorrow
> *I shan't* forget you.
> *They won't* be late.

Very often it goes with words such as *when, until, if* and *unless*; note that the verb following these is in the simple present:

> I'll give Tom this record *when I meet* him next week.
> I shan't leave *until you feel* better.
> You'll catch the bus *if you hurry.*
> Mr Brown will be angry *unless you stop* that noise.

Note (a) that 'until' = 'till' which is often used in conversation, and
(b) that 'unless' is a negative word, often meaning 'if . . . not':
> Mr Brown will be angry *if* you *don't* stop that noise.

Read this conversation and answer the questions below.

Sandra: Where will we spend our holidays this year, Mum?
Mother: Your father wants to go to the New Forest in Hampshire. We'll be there from May 10th until the end of the month, but I've no idea where we'll stay.

Sandra:

I think it will be fun if we go on a camping holiday. We'll take our
own tent and have our meals when we like. Perhaps we can camp
quite near the beach and then we'll go swimming every morning if
the sea is warm enough. We'll go on a boat-trip to the Isle of
Wight as well. It won't cost us much and it won't be too crowded
in May. It will be lovely sleeping in the fresh air with all those
wild ponies outside.

Mother:

Yes, but how long will it take to put up the tent every night? And
who will cut up the firewood, light the fire and cook the dinner?
We'll be so busy, there won't be enough time to visit the Isle of
Wight. It won't be a holiday for one member of the family and I
know who that will be! Besides, it will probably rain every day and
then what will we do? And I don't think those ponies will like
having us around; they'll probably knock our tent over every night.
No, I think it'll be better to stay in a Bed and Breakfast Guest
House. It'll be quite cheap and at least we shan't have any work to
do.

Sandra:

Oh, but that will be too much like living at home. If you don't like
camping, I'm sure you'll enjoy a holiday in a caravan. If we hire
one that's large enough, we'll have enough space to relax and be
comfortable.

Mother:

I don't think I'll get much comfort from a caravan. There won't be
enough room to sit down and I'm sure I'll bump my head
whenever I stand up. What an idea! I suppose you'll suggest we
stay in a houseboat next. That will be lovely! We can all enjoy being
cold and sea-sick.

Sandra:

Well, I don't know what else to suggest, Mum. I'm sure you will
never be happy unless we stay in a five-star hotel.

EXERCISE 42

Now choose the best answers:

1) Sandra thinks she will enjoy camping
   a) because she'll do her own cooking.
   b) because she'll feel free.
2) She'll go swimming
   a) if the sea isn't too cold.
   b) if the beach isn't too crowded.
3) If she has enough time
   a) she'll go riding.
   b) she'll swim to the Isle of Wight.
   c) she'll travel on a boat.

4) Her mother thinks
   a) it will rain all the time.
   b) there won't be enough time to do all the work.
   c) it won't be possible to visit the Isle of Wight.
5) Her mother says
   a) she won't go on a camping holiday with the family.
   b) she won't enjoy this kind of holiday.
   c) she doesn't know who will do the work.
6) Her mother thinks
   a) caravans are too large.
   b) the seats in caravans are too hard.
   c) caravans aren't big enough.
7) Her mother thinks a holiday in a houseboat will be
   a) enjoyable.
   b) expensive.
   c) horrible.
8) Which of the following are important to Sandra and which are important to her mother:
   a) feeling free *b)* exercise *c)* comfort *d)* low costs *e)* adventure
   f) fresh air *g)* relaxation *h)* a contrast to normal life?
9) How long will the family be away from home?
10) What in Sandra's opinion is the only way her mother will enjoy her holiday?

In this conversation you saw the words *too* and *enough.*
Look at these pictures:

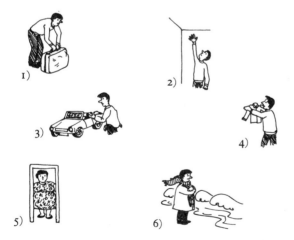

In picture 1, Mark is trying to lift a suitcase but he can't. Why not?
   a) Because it's *too heavy* for him to lift.
   b) Because he isn't *strong enough.*

EXERCISE 43

Give two answers for each question in the same way:

2) Why can't Mark touch the ceiling?   (high/tall)
3) Why can't he buy that sports-car?   (expensive/rich)
4) Why can't he wear that shirt?   (small/small)
5) Why can't the lady get through the doorway?   (narrow/slim)
6) Why can't he have a swim?   (cold/warm)

Remember the position of *enough*:

after an adjective	He isn't *rich enough*.
after an adverb	You aren't driving *fast enough*.
before a noun	He hasn't got *enough money*.

Very/rather/quite/fairly

Only use these words before adjectives and adverbs.

Here are Sandra's exam results with her teacher's comments:

Maths	98%	excellent
Physics	85%	very good
Chemistry	65%	quite good
History	60%	fairly good
Geography	50%	satisfactory
Art	35%	not good enough
Music	19%	rather poor
French	6%	very weak

Use *rather* as the negative form of *quite*:

This chair is is *quite* comfortable.
This chair is *rather* uncomfortable.

Certainty and uncertainty about the future

1. When you are *uncertain* about a future action use

May (or *might*) / *May not* (might not) + simple present

      It *might* rain tomorrow. = Perhaps it will rain.
      I *may* go to the cinema, I'm not sure. = Perhaps I'll go.
      They *might not* come. = Perhaps they won't come.

2. When you are *completely certain* (100% sure) use

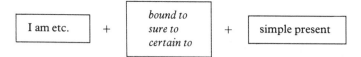

I am etc. + *bound to* / *sure to* / *certain to* + simple present

      John is standing outside in the rain without an umbrella.
      He's *bound/sure/certain to* get wet.

3. When you are certain something will happen *almost immediately* use

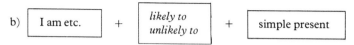

I am etc. + *about to* / *just going to* + simple present

      The football match has almost finished and the referee is looking at
      his watch. He's *about to/just going to* blow the whistle.
      Mary is standing on a diving-board. She is *about to/just going to*
      dive into the swimming-pool.

4. When you are *almost certain* about a future action (90% sure) use

a) *will + probably* + simple present, or

b) I am etc. + *likely to* / *unlikely to* + simple present

      David is bigger and stronger than Steve.
      He will/He'll probably win the boxing-match.
      He is/He's likely to win the boxing-match.
      He is/He's unlikely to lose the boxing-match.

EXERCISE 44

In this picture several things might happen. Examine it carefully and then answer the questions below, using one of the forms just explained.

1) The little boy is fishing. If he's lucky, he may *catch a fish.*
2) The branch isn't very strong. It may ___ .
3) If the branch breaks, the boy is likely to ___ ___ ___ ___ .
4) If he falls into the river, ___ ___ ___ get wet.
5) In the picture there is a bee. What do you think it may do? ___ ___ ___
   ___ ___ .
6) If it stings the man, he's likely to ___ ___ .
7) He ___ have to see a doctor.
8) What is the woman with the cigarette about to do? ___ ___ ___ ___
   ___ ___ .
9) What is the girl about to do with her sandwich? ___ ___ ___ ___
   ___ .
10) The sky is very dark and cloudy; it's about ___ ___ .
11) When it starts to rain, everyone ___ ___ hide under a tree or they ___
    run back to the car. They are ___ ___ continue having a picnic.

Some more pronouns:

everybody = everyone (all the people)
nobody = no one (not one of the people)
somebody = someone (a person – I don't know his name)
anybody = anyone (after 'not' and in questions)

Look at these sentences:
> When I went to the party, I saw twenty people. *Everybody was*
> dancing and *nobody was* sitting down. (= twenty people were
> dancing, the chairs were empty)

Note how a singular verb (*is, was, has*) is used after *everybody* and *everyone*.
> There is *someone* in the kitchen. (A person, but I don't know who it
> is)
> There isn't *anybody* in the dining-room.
> Is there *anybody* in the lounge?

Use *everything, nothing, something, anything* in the same way.

Note that a *thing* (an object – I don't know what it is) is 'countable', whereas *stuff*
(a substance – I don't know what) is 'uncountable':
> What's that *thing* in the girl's hand? It's a sandwich.
> What's that *stuff* in the bottle? It's lemonade.

EXERCISE 45

Look back at the picture of the picnic and complete these sentences using
everybody, nobody, etc.

1) ____ is sitting down or lying down.
2) ____ is standing up.
3) ____ is eating a sandwich.
4) ____ is talking.
5) Is ____ swimming? No, but ____ is fishing.
6) Is ____ sitting in the car? No, ____ is outside in the fresh air.
7) Has the boy caught ____ yet? No, but he hopes he will catch ____ soon.
8) Has the girl got ____ to eat? Yes, there is ____ in her hand.
9) Is the man lying down doing ____ ? No, he is doing ____ .
10) Has ____ got wet yet? No, it hasn't started raining yet but ____ is about to
    get wet.

Future in the past

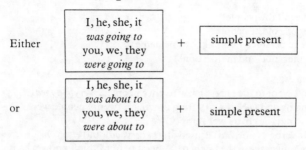

Either — I, he, she, it *was going to* you, we, they *were going to* + simple present

or — I, he, she, it *was about to* you, we, they *were about to* + simple present

Use this tense for an action which a person intended to do but which *didn't happen*. For example:

> When Mike was in Africa he *was going* to have a swim in the river but then he saw a crocodile and changed his mind. He went to a swimming-pool instead.

Did Mike want to have a swim in the river? Yes, he did. Did he enter the water? No, he didn't. Here is another example:

> Meg *was about* to cross the road when she saw a lorry coming, so she waited on the pavement.

Future continuous

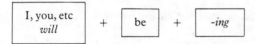

I, you, etc *will* + be + *-ing*

This time tomorrow, Mary *will be flying* between London and New York. Use this tense in the same way as the past continuous on page 44 (Yesterday at this time Mary *was flying* over the Alps) but in a future situation.

EXERCISE 46

Complete these sentences using either the future in the past or the future continuous.

1) I expect you'll find Sue in her office after lunch. She ___ ___ typing letters.
2) The cowboy ___ ___ ___ take out his revolver when the sheriff shot him.
3) Sheila ___ ___ ___ marry Bob, when she met his brother and married him instead.
4) I'm going away on holiday this evening, so tomorrow I ___ ___ working in the office; ___ ___ sitting on the beach instead.
5) Stella is working hard as an actress; in two years' time she hopes she ___ ___ living in Hollywood.
6) John ___ ___ ___ drink his wine when he saw a fly in his glass.
7) You'll recognise my sister at the party tomorrow; she ___ ___ wearing a blue and yellow dress.
8) I ___ ___ ___ answer the telephone when it stopped ringing.

Infinitive and gerund

When two verbs come together (separated either by a pronoun or preposition), the second verb can take different forms – the infinitive or the gerund.

1. The *infinitive* is the 'name' of the verb, the form by which most verbs are known. It usually has the word *to* in front of it, and describes an action or condition without itself needing a personal pronoun or further qualification:

> to work   to smoke   to help

When used in a sentence, where the infinitive follows another verb, you will generally see:

> My father *wants to work* in the garden.

But when the subject of 'work' is another person (not 'my father'), use a pronoun or noun before the infinitive:

> My father *wants me/us/Tom to work* in the garden.

The word *to* is omitted in some cases: after auxiliary verbs (such as *let*); after verbs expressing sensation (such as *see, feel*); after *make* and *help*. For example:

> Jane's father lets her smoke.
> Jane sees her father smoke.
> Jane's boss makes her work hard.
> Jane helps her mother cook dinner.

There are exceptions to the above – for example, the auxiliary verb *ought* needs *to*, and this word is also necessary when *see, make,* etc are used in the passive (see p. 69):

> Jane's father ought to stop her smoking.
> She was made to work hard.

2. The *gerund*, which is a 'verbal noun', has exactly the same form as the present participle ending in *-ing*:

> I enjoy *playing* tennis. I quite like *jogging*.
> She likes *being* an actress. She hates *singing*.

Notice how the gerunds *jogging* and *singing* have taken on the form of nouns.

Important: You should always use a gerund form for a verb immediately following a preposition:

> He left the restaurant *without* pay*ing*.
> They talked *about* buy*ing* a new car.
> I'm keen *on* sail*ing*.

The preposition 'to' can sometimes be confused with the *to* of an infinitive. When you see the word in the *going to* form (p. 26), or placed after *be, have, ought, used,* it is part of the following verb's infinitive. It can also be put after verbs such as *love, want, hope, like, hate* and others, when it represents a previously mentioned infinitive:

> Are you coming for a walk?
> I'd love *to* (= I'd love *to come*), but my feet hurt.

There are certain verbs and phrases after which you should use the gerund, rather than the infinitive. There are others where you may use either. There is no rule in English to show which goes with which.

The following points may help you.

1. These 'speaking' verbs are followed by the infinitive:

> John *asked/begged/persuaded/told/ordered* me to go away.

2. These verbs of future intention are followed by the infinitive:

> The criminal *hoped/wished/threatened/promised/wanted/waited* to kill the policeman.

3. These verbs must be followed by the gerund:

> John *avoids/considers/enjoys/keeps on/resents* working.
> He *anticipates/fancies/imagines/practises/suggests* doing it all day.

4. Use the gerund after these phrases:

> John is lazy and *can't stand* getting up in the morning (= he hates doing this). He says he *can't help* sleeping late (= he might not want to, but can't stop himself). Luckily his friend *doesn't mind* taking John to work in his car; he says *it's no use* waiting for a bus. John's boss says *it's not worth* paying him if he's always late.

EXERCISE 47

Maria is in hospital after a skiing accident. She has broken her leg. Two friends of hers are talking about her. Read the following conversation between Sally and Jane and put the verbs in brackets into the correct form (infinitive or gerund), if you think they need changing.

Sally: What's the matter, Jane?
Jane: I keep (think) about poor Maria in hospital. I begged her (stop) skiing down that steep slope.
Sally: You can never persuade Maria (do) anything; it's no use (try)!
Jane: I know. But I can't help (cry) when I think of her (lie) in bed all day.
Sally: It's no use (get) upset. How are we going to make her (feel) more cheerful?

Jane:	I know. Why don't we take her something to read?
Sally:	That's a good idea. What does she enjoy (read) most?
Jane:	I know she dislikes (look) at magazines and I don't think it's worth (take) any newspapers – she won't want (spend) all day (read) those.
Sally:	We must also avoid (take) adventure stories; we don't want her (have) another skiing accident!
Jane:	I believe she's very fond of (read) ghost stories.
Sally:	Yes, but they might prevent her from (sleep) at night. We want (make) her (feel) better, not worse! What about (go) to the library and (get) some good detective stories, Sherlock Holmes or Agatha Christie for example? They are easy to read and might help her (improve) her English. She might enjoy (read) some amusing short stories too, or perhaps (look) at some comics.
Jane:	Unfortunately, I don't belong to a Public Library.
Sally:	It's easy (join); it's only necessary (show) some proof of your home address.
Jane:	I see. Do you think it's worth (join) one?
Sally:	Yes, of course. It's free. Many libraries let you (take) out records and tapes as well.
Jane:	I think I'll go now. Would you mind (help) me (choose) something interesting for Maria?
Sally:	All right. But before (go), let me first (find) my library ticket.

EXERCISE 48

Does Jane keep forgetting about Maria? No, Jane keeps thinking about Maria.
Write out and correct the sentences in Exercise 48 like this example.

1) Maria can't stand reading ghost stories.
2) Detective stories are difficult to read.
3) It's expensive to join a library.
4) Sally wants to take Maria some adventure stories.
5) Jane says Maria enjoys reading magazines.
6) Sally thinks ghost stories will help Maria sleep at night.

EXERCISE 49

Give short answers to these questions.
1) What does Maria enjoy reading?
2) What does Maria dislike reading?
3) How do we know Jane feels sorry for Maria?
4) Why was Maria skiing so fast?
5) Which of the three girls is:
    a) sensitive?   b) practical?   c) obstinate?

Special verbs (modals or auxiliaries)

1. *Have to* and *must*: Showing that an action is *necessary*.

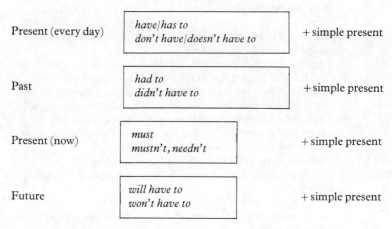

Present (every day)	*have/has to* *don't have/doesn't have to*	+ simple present
Past	*had to* *didn't have to*	+ simple present
Present (now)	*must* *mustn't, needn't*	+ simple present
Future	*will have to* *won't have to*	+ simple present

In really urgent situations use *have got to* instead of *must*.

> Claire works as an air hostess. Every day she *has to wear* a uniform. She *has to make* the passengers feel comfortable and she *has to serve* meals, but she *doesn't have to cook* anything and she *doesn't have to clean* the plane in the airport.

> Claire used to work in a bank. She *didn't have to wear* a uniform then, but she *had to start* work at the same time every day and she always *had to work* in the same place.

> It's 7.15 pm and a passenger has just called her. He feels ill. She *must take* him a glass of water and an aspirin and she *must give* him a blanket. She *needn't give* him any dinner, because he isn't hungry.

> Now the plane has serious engine trouble. The pilot *has got to make* an emergency landing. Claire *has got to be* calm. The passengers *have got to put on* their life-jackets.

EXERCISE 50

Tommy is a soldier in the army. What does he have to do every day?
The things that he has to do are listed in Exercise 50. Write sentences for each of these, like the example below:

make/bed   *He has to make his bed.*
1) clean/rifle
2) polish/boots
3) wear/uniform
4) get up/6am
5) peel/potatoes
6) salute/officers

EXERCISE 51

Now Tommy is fighting in a battle. What must he do?

keep/head down   *He must keep his head down.*

1) load/rifle
2) fire at/enemy
3) put on/helmet

Someone has shot his friend in the arm. What has Tommy got to do?

4) make/a bandage   *He has got to . . .*
5) give/water
6) get/to hospital

EXERCISE 52

Now he is on leave (= on holiday)

get up/early   *He needn't get up early.*

1) clean/shoes
2) wear/uniform
3) cook/breakfast
4) carry/rifle

2. Showing an action is the right thing to do

ought to should	oughtn't to shouldn't	+ simple present

Compare these two sentences:

a) I *must visit* Aunt Mabel because she is very ill.

b) I *ought to* visit Aunt Mabel because she is feeling lonely. (= it is not necessary to go but *my conscience* tells me to).

EXERCISE 53

Look at the pictures above. What do you think Johnny ought to do in these situations? For example, in the bigger picture an old lady is about to cross the road:
He ought to help the old lady to cross the road.

Now complete the exercise, using *ought to* and the verb in brackets ( ).

1) picking up £5 note which has dropped out of man's pocket   (give)
2) sitting in a crowded bus – old lady standing up   (offer)
3) eating sweets, hungry child staring at him   (give)
4) night, clock 11pm, watching TV   (go to bed)

3. *Advising* a course of action

a) An immediate action
| had better |
| had better not |
+ simple present

    I've got a stomach-ache.
    You *had* (You'd) *better* take some medicine.

b) An action going into the future
| should |
+ simple present

    I'm getting very fat.
    You *should* eat less. You *should* go on a diet.

EXERCISE 54

James looks worried. What do you think he had better do?

    phone/zoo   *He had better phone the zoo.*

1) warn/neighbours
2) close/the windows
3) lock/all the doors
4) call/the police
5) give/something to eat

EXERCISE 55

James' grandfather has a very bad temper. What do you think they had better do?

    make/noise   *They had better not make a noise.*

1) play/record-player
2) turn on/television
3) talk/too loudly
4) slam/door
5) open/window

EXERCISE 56

Margaret wants to be an actress. She is going to meet a famous producer next week. Give her some advice before she goes.

    wear/fashionable dress   *You should wear a fashionable dress.*

1) go/hairdresser
2) put on/make-up
3) stop/smoking
4) buy/elegant shoes
5) look/more cheerful
6) wear/contact lenses

4. *Warning* or *order not* to do something

must not/mustn't

+ simple present

You *mustn't touch* that electric wire.
You *mustn't tell* this secret to anyone.

EXERCISE 57

Jimmy is going to a zoo for the first time in his life. What are some of the things his mother tells him he mustn't do?
Jimmy is standing too close to the animals.   *You mustn't go too near the animals.*

1) Jimmy wants to stroke the lion.   *You mustn't . . .*
2) He is about to give the monkeys some bananas.   *You mustn't . . .*
3) He is trying to touch a snake.   *You mustn't . . .*
4) He wants to throw his ball at the seal.   *You mustn't . . .*
5) He is trying to pull the tiger's tail.   *You mustn't . . .*

5. *Criticism*

shouldn't

+ simple present

You *shouldn't be* rude.
You *shouldn't drive* fast in a city.

The past form is very common.

should have *shouldn't have*

+ past participle

You *should have written* a letter to your mother. (= but you didn't)
I *shouldn't have eaten* that bad fish. (= but I did and now I'm ill)

Mr Biggs is not a good cook. He wears his suit in the kitchen, and he manages to drop the eggs on the floor. Instead of putting the plates on the table he puts them on the cooker, and he even puts salt in the milk!

EXERCISE 58

Mrs Biggs doesn't think her husband is a very good cook. Write out her criticisms.
      make/mess   *You shouldn't make a mess in the kitchen.*

1) wear/suit
2) drop eggs/floor
3) put plates/cooker
4) put salt/milk

EXERCISE 59

Mrs Biggs is very cross with her husband. But it is too late to worry now; he has spoilt her breakfast.

How does she criticise him?

    suit/dirty/apron *You shouldn't have made your suit dirty; you should have put on an apron.*

1) broken/plates/table *You shouldn't . . .*
2) burnt/toast/watched it *You shouldn't . . .*
3) let milk/boil over/watched it *You shouldn't . . .*
4) let sink/overflow/turned off tap *You shouldn't . . .*

6. *Inference*

Present	*must be* *can't be*	+ present participle (-ing) + adjective
Past	*must have been* *must have*	+ past participle/noun/adjective + past participle

This use of *must* is completely different from that described in paragraph 1 on page 62. Here it shows that I think or *assume* something is true.

    Bert's nose is red and he can't walk properly. Why? *He's just come out of a pub. He must be drunk. He can't be sober.*

EXERCISE 60

Answer these questions using *must* and *can't* in this way.

      What is Mr James?   *He must be a businessman.*

      What is Steve?   *He can't be a businessman. He must be a student.*

1) Mr James has a big car.   ___ ___ ___ *rich.*

2) Steve hasn't got a car.   ___ ___ ___ *poor.*

3) How old is Mr James?   *He must* ___ ___ ___ . *He can't be less* ___ ___ .

4) How old is Steve?   *He must* ___ ___ ___ . *He can't be more* ___ ___ .

5) Mr James doesn't have to drive a car. Why not?   ___ ___ ___ *a chauffeur.*

6) Why do you think Steve looks tired?   ___ ___ *read* ___ ___ ___ ___ .

7) Why is he going into a restaurant?   ___ ___ ___ *hungry.*

8) Why is Mr James very fat?   ___ ___ *eat* ___ ___ .

9) What kind of house does Mr James live in?   ___ ___ ___ ___ *a mansion.*

10) Why does Steve have to wear glasses?   ___ ___ ___ *short-sighted.*

The passive form

This is formed by using a tense from the verb 'to be' + the past participle of the main verb + *by*.

Look at these sentences which are in the past tense:
> A policeman arrested my brother
> A thief has stolen my watch

The passive is used when you want to show that the object of the sentence is more important than the subject. For example, the *objects* of the above sentences – my brother and my watch – are more important than a policeman or a thief (the *subjects*). To show that importance it is better to mention them first; so we now have:
> My brother *was arrested by* a policeman.
> My watch *was stolen by* a thief

These sentences are in the *passive* tense. In the passive tense, the subjects are changed into the objects; they go after the verb and are introduced by the word 'by'.

Look carefully at the sentences below. Line B gives the passive form of the tense in Line A.

A The nurse gives Tom an injection every day
B Tom is given an injection by the nurse every day

A The nurse is giving Tom an injection now
B Tom is being given an injection by the nurse now

A The nurse gave Tom an injection yesterday
B Tom was given an injection by the nurse yesterday

A The nurse has given Tom an injection today
B Tom has been given an injection by the nurse today

A The nurse will give/is going to give Tom an injection tomorrow
B Tom will be given/is going to be given an injection by the nurse tomorrow

A The nurse should/must give Tom an injection soon
B Tom should/must be given an injection by the nurse soon

The phrase using the preposition 'by' (in the example above 'by the nurse') can often be left out, e.g.

> A policeman arrested my brother →
> My brother was arrested (by a policeman)

The passive tense often implies the 'by' phrase; therefore it is unnecessary to repeat it.

After certain verbs 'with' is used instead of 'by':

> Air filled the balloon→
> The balloon was filled *with* air

EXERCISE 61

In the following sentences answer each question in the passive form, using the information given. For example, in 1) a the answer would be: *tyres are made of rubber.*

1) What are these things made of?
   a) tyres/rubber   b) sweaters/wool   c) mirrors/glass   d) shoes/leather

2) What are these things made from?
   a) bread/flour   b) wine/grapes   c) omelettes/eggs   d) porridge/oats

3) What are these things usually kept in?
   a) car/garage   b) dresses/wardrobe   c) pound notes/wallet
   d) matches/matchbox

4) What are these things used for?
   a) soap/washing   b) kettle/boiling water   c) bricks/building
   d) toothpaste/cleaning teeth

5) Where were these famous people born?
   a) Napoleon/Corsica   b) Shakespeare/England   c) President
      Roosevelt/America

6) Which countries were discovered by
   a) Pedro Cabral/Brazil   b) Columbus/America
   c) Captain Cooke/New Zealand

7) What was invented by
   a) Stephenson/railway engine   b) Fleming/penicillin   c) Baird/television

8) Which famous person was assassinated in
   a) 1914/Archduke Ferdinand of Austria   b) 1948/Ghandi
   c) 1963/John F. Kennedy

9) Where are these types of dress worn?
   a) kimonos/Japan   b) kilts/Scotland   c) ponchos/Mexico
   d) saris/India

10) Where is this type of food most commonly eaten?
    a) paella/Spain   b) stroganov/Russia   c) ghoulash/Hungary
    d) frogs' legs/France

EXERCISE 62

Change these sentences into the passive using the sentences on page 69 to help you. Follow this example:

> Mary has fed the baby twice today→
> *The baby has been fed (by Mary) twice today*

It is not necessary to put in 'by her' with each sentence.
1) She usually feeds him four times a day.
2) She has just taken him into the bathroom.
3) She is giving him a bath.
4) She ought to wash his hair.
5) She is going to dry him in a moment.
6) She must cut his hair soon.
7) She'll take him out in his pram if it stops raining.
8) She must keep him warm.
9) She'll put him to bed at 7 o'clock.
10) He never lets her rest (use 'allow').

Passive with 'to have' [the 'causative' have]
This is a special passive form which shows that *another person* is involved. It is formed by using the verb

> 'to have' + object + past participle of main verb

Look at these sentences; the second is the passive of the first:

> Someone is going to cut the baby's hair →
> The baby is going to have his hair cut

EXERCISE 63

Change these sentences into the passive form following the example given:

> Someone is going to repair my car →
> I'm going to have my car repaired

Someone is going to
1) paint my house for me
2) clean my windows
3) mend my shoes
4) cut my grass for me
5) manicure my nails
6) send my baggage to my hotel
7) dry clean my suit
8) test my eyes for me

Joining sentences

The sentence, clause and phrase

This chapter shows you how to write complex sentences and join sentences together.
First note the meaning of these words:

A sentence	=	a complete statement, command, or question, *with a verb*: She looked tired. I saw the boy. Do not go out. Are you keen on golf?

A clause	=	*a part* of a sentence *with a verb*: She looked tired *when I arrived*. I saw the boy *who gave me the book*.

A phrase	=	*a part* of a sentence *without a verb*: I saw the boy *in the kitchen*. Do not go out *without an umbrella*.

You can join two sentences by using a semi-colon (;) or a conjunction – the most common of which is *and*. Never use a comma (,) between two sentences.

He drank a bottle of wine; he drank some whisky as well.
He drank some wine *and* fell asleep.

A comma may be used between sentence and clause especially if the latter is a long one. It *must* be used when the relative clause (see below) does not define the noun it follows, otherwise a different meaning could be assumed:

I saw the boy, who gave me the book.
I saw the boy who gave me the book.

In the second of these examples, I'm making it clear that I saw one boy in particular – the one who gave me the book.

Relative (or 'describing') clauses

These describe or give information about the preceding noun. Use them in the ways shown in the following paragraphs 1–5. In a describing clause, the noun referred to is replaced by one of the *relative pronouns* shown below, depending on whether it is a person, an animal or a thing:

people →	who whom that

people and animals →	whose

things and animals →	which that

things →	whose

1. Giving definitions

EXERCISE 64

1) What is a baker?   *A baker is someone who sells bread.*
Write sentences in the same way:
     a) What is a butcher?   b) a chemist?   c) a newsagent?   d) a greengrocer?
     e) a bus-conductor?
2) What is an air-hostess?   *An air-hostess is someone who looks after*
    passengers in a plane.
     a) What is a nurse?   b) a baby-sitter?   c) a caretaker?   d) a courier?
     e) a cloakroom attendant?
3) What is a sheep?   *A sheep is an animal which gives us wool.*
     a) What is a cow?   b) a hen?   c) a silkworm?   d) a mink?   e) a pig?
4) *India is a country which is famous for tea.*
Write similar sentences for:
     a) Brazil   b) Saudi Arabia   c) Ghana   d) Ireland   e) Jamaica

2. Replacing the object
Look at these sentences:
        Here's the man. You met *him* at the party.
        Here's the man *whom* you met at the party.

Notice the changes: a) the sentences are joined with *whom*
                 b) the pronoun *him* has disappeared
(i) you may use 'that' instead of 'whom'
(ii) 'who' instead of 'whom' is common in conversation
(iii) very often the relative pronoun is omitted, especially in conversation:
        Here's the man you met at the party.

Another example:
        Here's Helen's new dress. She has never worn *it* before.
        Here's Helen's new dress, *which* she has never worn before.
Special note:
In everyday, conversational English, prepositions usually go at the end of the
sentence and *not before* the relative pronoun.
        George is the player whom I'm talking about.
        Not 'about whom I'm talking'.

EXERCISE 65

Complete these sentences like this:
Sue didn't dance with Tim. *Jack is the boy (whom) she danced with.*

1) She didn't speak to Tim. *Jack is*__ __ __ __ __ .
2) She isn't fond of Tim. __ __ __ __ __ __ __ __ .
3) She didn't shout at Tim. __ __ __ __ __ __ __ .
4) She doesn't feel sorry for Tim. __ __ __ __ __ __ __ __ .
5) She didn't argue with Tim. __ __ __ __ __ __ __ .
6) She didn't play tennis with Tim. __ __ __ __ __ __ __ __ .
7) She didn't talk about Tim. __ __ __ __ __ __ __ .
8) She isn't tired of Tim. __ __ __ __ __ __ __ __ .

3. Extra information (non-defining)

Look at these sentences:

> Sally, who is 21, is going to appear on television.
> St Ives, which is a lovely seaport, is famous for its artists.

In these sentences Sally's age or the beauty of St Ives is something extra and not the main point being made.

In this use of the relative –
a) you must use commas before and after the clause
b) you must use 'who' or 'which', *not* 'that'

4. Possessive forms *(whose, of whom, of which)*

whose is used to replace the pronouns *his, her, its, their* as in these examples:

> Last night I met Joan. *Her* mother is a famous actress.
> Last night I met Joan, *whose* mother is a famous actress.
> Here are the children. *Their* teacher is away.
> Here are the children *whose* teacher is away.

of whom replaces *of them* and *of which* replaces *of it.*

> There were 30 guests at the party. *Most of them* were teenagers.
> There were 30 guests at the party, *most of whom* were teenagers.
> Mary brought in a cake. She gave *some of it* to the child.
> Mary brought in a cake, *some of which* she gave to the child.

5. Use of *that*

That can replace *who* or *which* – see the examples in paragraphs 1 and 2 on page 73. Use it (a) after a superlative form, and (b) after 'all', 'every':

> This is the best hotel *that* I know.
> I agree with all *that* you say.

EXERCISE 66

Form one sentence from each of the following questions, using a relative form:

1) Brighton is a delightful town. It is situated on the South Coast.
2) It was made famous by George IV. He built the extraordinary Chinese Pavilion.

3) The coastline looks beautiful from the beach. The beach is covered with pebbles.
4) There are a lot of shellfish. You can buy them under the promenade.
5) There are two piers. One of them has been badly damaged.
6) The Lanes is a place behind the Palace Pier. It is famous for antiques.
7) The Aquarium and Model Railway are also popular. They are alongside the beach.
8) There are a lot of young people in Brighton. Many of them are students. Their university is outside the town.
9) There are also a few eccentric people. Some of them are actors.
10) Graham Greene has been to many strange places. He is a writer. He thinks Brighton is the strangest.
(Graham Greene . . . thinks Brighton is the strangest place . . .)

Time clauses

when =	as (just as) an exact point in time	while (whilst) = a continuous period

Notice the difference between these sentences:
As he was driving along the road, he noticed a lion on the pavement. (one action)
While he was driving along the road, he was smoking a cigar. (continuous action)
while + verb = during/throughout + phrase

EXERCISE 67

Change these sentences as in this example:
Brian fell asleep during the film.
= *Brian fell asleep while he was watching the film.*
1) I hurt my knee during the football match.
2) She felt nervous during her driving-lesson.
3) He was ill throughout his holiday.
4) During the history lesson he fell asleep.

Now change *while* to *during*:
5) Let's tidy the office, while he is absent.
6) While he was at the party, he got drunk.
7) He felt sick while he was watching the play.

Remember . . . *during* often means 'once', 'in the course of', and *throughout* means 'the whole time':
During his holiday he was stung by a bee.
Throughout the holiday he was sick. (= every day)

Cause clauses

These are linked to the rest of the sentence by the words *because, as, since* and *so*, or the sentence may begin with such a clause. For example:

> You'd better put a coat on *as* you're cold.
> You'd better put a coat on *since* you're cold.
> You'd better put a coat on *because* you're cold.

> *As/since* you're cold, you'd better put a coat on.
> You're cold, *so* you'd better put a coat on.

Notice that *because* and *so* can only go in *the middle* of the sentence and not at the beginning.

EXERCISE 68

Change these sentences using *so* instead of *as*:

> As he's tired, he's going to bed early.
> = *He's tired, so he's going to bed early.*

1) As he's deaf, he can't hear you.
2) As he's short-sighted, he can't see you.
3) As he's short, he can't reach the top shelf.
4) As he's very fat, he can't run fast.

Now change the sentences using *as* instead of *so*:

5) I've overslept, so I'll be late.
6) He's very mean, so he won't buy you a present.
7) She's very kind, so I'm sure she'll help you.
8) The children are very clever, so I expect they'll pass their exams.

With phrases use *because of* or *owing to* (= in view of), and note also the use of *due to*, which generally requires another verb after the noun:

> I can't play tennis *because of* the rain.
> I can't play tennis *owing to* the rain.
> I can't play tennis *due to* the awful weather we've been having.

EXERCISE 69

Change these phrases into cause clauses as in the example using *as, since* or *because*:

> The football match has been cancelled *owing to the snow.*
> The football match has been cancelled *because it's been snowing.*

The football match has been cancelled owing to

1) a rail strike
2) a flu epidemic
3) the pitch being wet
4) a dispute with the manager

Surprise clauses (clauses of concession)

although, though, even, though
Look at these sentences:
> Bert hit him. Jim laughed.
> It was snowing. Jim went for a swim.

In each case Jim behaves in an unexpected or surprising way. To join these sentences use *although* before the first of the two actions:
> *Although* Bert hit him, Jim laughed.

When it is a very big surprise use *even though*:
> *Even though* it was snowing Jim went for a swim.

With phrases use *in spite of* or *despite*:
> *Despite/In spite of* the snow Jim went for a swim.

There is no real difference between these; *in spite of* is perhaps more often used nowadays.

EXERCISE 70   In this, change the *in spite of/despite* phrases into clauses linked by *although*. For example: Sue is fond of Steve, despite his ugliness. = *Sue is fond of Steve, although he is ugly*.

Sue is fond of Steve
1) in spite of his rudeness.
2) despite his bad temper.
3) despite his stupidity.
4) in spite of his untidy appearance.
5) in spite of his meanness.
6) despite his unpopularity.

Now change *although* to *in spite of* or *despite*
I'm going to play tennis
7) although it's raining.
8) although I have a cold.
9) even though I have a broken arm.
10) although the doctor ordered me not to.
11) although the weather is awful.

Clauses of precaution

in case
Look at this sentence:
> It might rain, so you had better take an umbrella.

This can be put in another way:
> You had better take an umbrella *in case* it rains.

EXERCISE 71

Imagine you are going on a walking holiday in the mountains. What do you think you had better take in case you get thirsty? (Answer: a can of water)

You had also better take
1) a map in case *you get lost*.
2) some matches in case ___ ___ ___ ___ ___ ___ .

3) a thick sweater in case ___ ___ ___ .
4) some bandages in case ___ ___ ___ .
5) some sandwiches in case ___ ___ ___ .
6) a watch in case ___ ___ ___ ___ ___ ___ .

Clauses of purpose

in order to, in order not to, so as to, so as not to

These phrases introduce the reason or purpose of an action. For example:

Hugh is going to Spain. Why?
In order to/So as to learn Spanish.
Meg has turned the record-player off. Why?
So as not to/In order not to wake up her grandmother.

EXERCISE 72
In this next exercise, sentences *a–h* are clauses of purpose, or reasons why Jill is doing the action described in sentences 1–8. Write all of them down, matching each action with the correct reason.
1) Jill is going on a diet
2) She is having music lessons
3) She's putting on some sun-tan lotion
4) She's learning Russian
5) She's driving very carefully
6) She's looking through a pair of binoculars
7) She's running
8) She's saving up
a) in order to be an interpreter.
b) so as to catch the bus.
c) so as to lose weight.
d) in order to buy a car.
e) so as to see the race more clearly.
f) in order not to have an accident.
g) so as not to get sunburnt.
h) in order to be a pianist.

Now complete sentences 9–13 using the same forms and putting sensible reasons. For example: Mary wears a thick sweater so as to keep warm.

9) She wears a watch in order to ___ ___ ___ .
10) She wears a raincoat ___ ___ ___ ___ ___ .
11) She wears gloves ___ ___ ___ ___ ___ ___ ___ .
12) She wears glasses ___ ___ ___ ___ ___ .
13) She wears make-up ___ ___ ___ ___ ___ ___ .

Emphatic forms
so . . . that, such . . . that

Look at these two sentences:

Max is very rich. He has four large cars.
To emphasise that Max has four cars because he is very rich join the sentences like this:

Max is *so* rich *that* he has four large cars.

Further examples of when to use these emphatic forms follow:

Janet is *so* beautiful a pianist *that* everyone admires her
Janet plays the piano *so* well *that* everyone admires her
Janet has *so* much skill *that* everyone admires her
Janet knows *so* many tunes *that* everyone admires her
Janet is *such* a beautiful pianist *that* everyone admires her
Janet knows *such* a lot of tunes *that* everyone admires her

EXERCISE 73

Join these sentences together using *so* or *such . . . that*

1) I'm very tired. I can't keep my eyes open.
2) This suit is very expensive. He cannot afford it.
3) There's a lot of noise here. I can't hear you.
4) There are too many people here. I can't move.
5) The coffee was awful. I couldn't drink it.
6) She has eaten a lot of icecream. She feels sick.
7) I'm very hungry. I could eat a horse.
8) He has drunk a large amount of beer. He can't walk properly.

Complete the blanks with the same forms:

9) I've eaten ___ ___ cakes and ___ ___ lot of jelly that I feel ill.
10) He earns ___ ___ money that he can afford three holidays a year.
11) He skis ___ fast and with ___ grace that he'll win the competition.
12) He was ___ surprised to see me that he fell off his chair.

Conditional or 'if' clauses

Use these clauses in the following ways:

1. To show actions which are probable or certain in the future.

If is often replaced with one of these emphatic forms:

so long as, provided (that), as long as

Occasionally you may hear *providing (that)* in conversation, but the better form is *provided (that)*. The word *that* is often omitted.

Remember . . . these clauses are normally in the simple present tense + 'will' 'can' in the main part of the sentence. For example:

I'll let you drive my car *so long as* you promise to be careful.
You can go to the party *provided that* you wear a suit.

EXERCISE 74

Form sentences of your own in the same way:

lend you £5/*pay me back tomorrow*
I'll lend you £5 as long as you pay me back tomorrow.

1) use my phone/*don't talk too long*
2) borrow my umbrella/*give it back next week*
3) ride my horse/*don't jump over any hedges*

4) go for a swim/*don't go out too far*
5) have an icecream/*eat it slowly*
6) sit behind me on the motor-bike/*hold on tight*

2. To show an imaginary (or hypothetical) situation.
In this, form the '*if*' clause with the simple past tense and the main clause with *would*.

> If I *lived* on the moon, I *would* be happy.
> I *would* go to Peking, if I *knew* Chinese.

With the verb 'to be' it is better to use *were* instead of *was* after I, he, she, it.

> If I *were* you, I *would* buy a new car.

EXERCISE 75

To help you remember this form, here is a short personality test. Copy down each situation and then choose one of the answers *a–e* which applies to yourself. See page 123 for an assessment of your answers.
What would you do *if*:
1) you saw a snake?
   you saw a bank-robber?
   you saw a ghost?
   you saw a creature from another planet?
   you saw a huge spider?
2) you found a burglar in your house?
   you found a shoplifter in a store?
   you found a hijacker in a plane?
   you found an escaped prisoner in your car?
   you found a madman on the bus?

   Answers
a) I would run away.
b) I would scream.
c) I would attack it/him.
d) I would pay no attention.
e) I would watch what it/he did.

Note: *I would* etc is sometimes contracted to *I'd*; always use the contracted form *wouldn't* in the negative.

EXERCISE 76

Expand these words into sentences as in the example:
> If/I have a million pounds/buy a yacht
> *If I had a million pounds, I'd buy a yacht.*
1) If/the pupils work harder/pass their exams.
2) If/I am the Prime Minister/cut taxes.
3) If/you drive more slowly/not have so many accidents.
4) If/I live on a desert island/build my own house.
5) If/you are an astronaut/be very lonely.
6) Be an interpreter/if/I know Russian.

7) Drive a taxi/if/he has a driving-licence.
8) Not annoy his friends/if/he not phone them late at night.
9) Go to university/if/I am you.
10) Go mad/if/I have a job repairing roads.

3. Another use of the conditional clause is to show that someone is *wishing* something. *I wish* (meaning 'It would be very nice if') is another imaginary form. It is used three ways:
a) *Present* or '*now*' wish + simple past
    I wish I *knew* how to play the guitar.
b) *Future* wish + would
    I wish it *would* stop snowing.
c) *Past* wish + had (idea of *regret*)
    I wish I *had* invited Sheila to my party (but I didn't).

EXERCISE 77

Here are three examples of each type – fill in the spaces with the correct verb:
1) a) I wish I ____ Chinese; it is a difficult language to learn.
   b) He wishes he ____ a higher salary.
   c) Do you wish you ____ a pop-star?
2) a) I wish it ____ stop raining.
   b) Stan loves Sue and wishes she ____ write to him.
   c) I wish the government ____ cut taxes.
3) a) She wishes she ____ gone to university.
   b) I wish I ____ eaten that bad fish; I feel ill.
   c) Do you wish you ____ stayed at home?

Now think of yourself: What do you wish you had? What do you wish you could do? What do you wish you had done when you were young? (Give three or four examples for each.)
Imagine you are on a desert island: What would you do? What would you eat? What would you wear? How would you escape? Where would you live? Would you be happy?

4. The 'impossible condition' – thinking about or regretting actions in the past. Here, use an '*if*' clause with the past perfect tense and *would have*:
        If you *had come* to my party last week, you *would have* met Sue.
        I *wouldn't have* been ill, if I *hadn't eaten* those peaches.
In these sentences the person *didn't* go to the party so he didn't meet Sue. I *was* ill and I regret eating the peaches.

EXERCISE 78

Look back at Exercise 76 and expand the same words into sentences – but write them in the past form. For example:
1) If the pupils *had worked* harder, they *would have passed* their exams.
2) If I ____ Prime Minister ____
and so on, down to 10)

Connecting words

There are a lot of these words (called **conjunctions**) in English, and your dictionary will help you learn their precise meaning. Groups of the most common ones are explained here. Remember that conjunctions go at the *beginning* of a sentence or in the *middle* between two main clauses.

1. Comparisons:

Here are some facts about the Burns family:

	Mr Burns	Mrs Burns	Sandra	Derek
age	48	48	16	20
hair	dark-brown	blonde	blonde	fair
size	well-built	slim	slim	rather fat
weight	13 stone	$7\frac{1}{2}$ stone	$7\frac{1}{2}$ stone	$13\frac{1}{2}$ stone
eyes	brown	green	green	brown
hobbies	gardening, theatre, old cars	gardening, theatre, knitting	pop music, tennis	pop music, tennis

1a. *the same . . . as/as . . . as/similar . . . to*

We have already practised comparisons between different things or people (see page 23): *Derek is older than Sandra.* How do we compare the ages of Mr and Mrs Burns? Mrs Burns isn't older than her husband; she isn't younger either.

> She is *the same age as* her husband.
> She is *as old as* her husband.

EXERCISE 79

Make comparisons in the same way:
1) Mrs Burns' hair is blonde. Her daughter's hair is the same . . .
2) Mrs Burns is slim. Her daughter is as . . .
3) Mrs Burns weighs $7\frac{1}{2}$ stone. Sandra is the same . . .
4) Sandra has the same colour eyes . . .
5) Derek . . . eyes . . . father
6) Sandra has the same hobbies . . .

Has Mr Burns got the same hobbies as his wife?

> No, not exactly the same.   He has *similar hobbies to* his wife.

Answer in the same way:
7) Is Derek's hair the same colour as his sister's?
8) Is Derek the same size as his father?
9) Is his weight exactly the same as his father's?

1b. *so/neither/nor/neither . . . nor*

These are used to apply a statement to a second person or thing. Use *neither, nor* and *neither . . . nor* only in negative situations:

> Mr Burns is 48; *so* is his wife.
> Mr Burns hasn't got green eyes; *neither* (or *nor*) has his son.
> *Neither* Mr Burns *nor* his son has green eyes.

Complete these sentences:

10) Sandra has blonde hair; so . . .
11) Derek isn't slim; neither . . .
12) Mrs Burns weighs $7\frac{1}{2}$ stone; so . . .
13) Sandra doesn't like gardening; nor . . .
14) Mr Burns likes going to the theatre; so . . .
15) Sandra hasn't got brown eyes; . . .
16) Derek is fond of tennis; . . .

1c. *both/neither/all/none/like*

Mrs Burns resembles (looks like) her daughter in several ways:

> *Both of them* are slim and blonde.
> *Both* Mrs Burns *and* Sandra are slim and blonde

Mr Burns and Derek are different from Mrs Burns and Sandra:

> *Neither of them* is slim or blonde.
> *Neither* Mr Burns *nor* Derek is slim or blonde.

Notice that *of* must be put before a pronoun, and that when you mention names you must use *both . . . and* or *neither . . . nor*. The verb following *neither . . . nor* should be in the singular.

Whereas *both* and *neither* refer to two people or things, use *all* or *none* for more than this number:

> *All* of the Burns family are adults.
> *None* of them are young children.

EXERCISE 80

Now complete these sentences:

1) . . . have brown eyes.
2) . . . like tennis.
3) Neither Mrs Burns nor Sandra . . .
4) . . . are more than 15 years old.
5) . . . have black eyes.

To state a general resemblance, use *like*.

> Sandra is *like* her mother.

In what way is she like her mother? They both have green eyes and blonde hair. This means that Sandra *looks like* her mother.

84

EXERCISE 81

Choose a verb from the following list and make sentences in the same way: taste, feel, sound, look, smell, drive, talk

1) This ___ like cheese.
2) This ___ like chocolate.
3) This ___ like cotton wool.
4) That parrot ___ ___ an old woman.
5) Eels ___ ___ snakes.
6) Tom ___ his car ___ a maniac.
7) That ___ ___ Susan's voice.

Note the use of *as if*, *as though*, when only a general impression is given:

> It looks *as if* it's going to rain. (The sky suggests this).
> He drives *as though* he were in a race.

2. Conjunctions of **addition**:

and/besides/moreover/as well

Use *besides* when the sentence has a negative idea, and *moreover* with a positive idea:

> I can't play football because I've hurt my leg. I have an exam tomorrow. = *Besides*, I have an exam tomorrow.
> He is a great football player. He's the captain of his team.
> = *Moreover*, he's the captain of his team.

3. **Alternatives:**

or/or else/either . . . or/neither . . . nor/otherwise/whether . . . or

a) *or = and*, when following a negative verb:
> She can type *and* cook. She can't knit *or* sew.

b) *or else*. Usually used with a threat or warning:
> Put your hands up *or else* I'll shoot.
> = I'll shoot you if you don't put your hands up.

c) *either . . . or*. This is an emphatic form. Notice that the position of *either* is before the verb but after the special verb:
> You can *either* come out with us *or* you can stay at home.

d) *neither . . . nor*. The same as (c) but used in negative sentences.

e) *otherwise*. Indicates an alternative course of action:
> We'll go to the theatre if there are any seats left, *otherwise* we'll go to a Greek restaurant.
> = We'll go to a restaurant if there aren't any seats left.

f) *whether . . . or*. This is used after a verb of thinking or speaking, in a negative or question form:
> Can you tell me *whether* the match is going to be played *or* has it been cancelled?

4. Contrasting statements:

but/however/nevertheless/nonetheless

Use *but* in joining two contrasting statements of equal weight. When the second statement is surprising, replace *but* with one of the other words. Never put '. . . but, however, . . .'

> I enjoy swimming *but* I dislike sailing.
> John has been very naughty; *however*, his father isn't going to punish him.
> I know you're tired and hungry. *Nevertheless*, I think you should help us put up the tent.

5. Giving a list:

first of all/to start with/then/after that/last of all/to end with

What did you have for dinner last night, Mary?
First of all (or *To start with*) I had a slice of melon. *Then* I had some onion soup, *then* I had some fish; *after that* I had a steak. *Then* I had some pudding, and *to end with* (or *last of all*) I had coffee and Turkish delight.

EXERCISE 82

Complete these sentences choosing a link-word from those listed in 2, 3, 4 and 5 above:
1) Don't play with that knife ___ ___ you'll cut yourself.
2) Mike is very intelligent and worked extremely hard; ___ he failed his exam.
3) Tom went sight-seeing in London this morning. ___ ___ ___ he went to St. Paul's, ___ he went to the Old Bailey, ___ ___ he saw the Crown Jewels in the Tower of London and ___ ___ ___ he had lunch in a pub by the river.
4) We can ___ play tennis ___ go rowing on the river ___ we can't go to the skating-rink because it's too far from here. ___ it's always crowded on Saturday.
5) I have no idea ___ Chris wants to get married ___ remain a bachelor.
6) I hope there isn't a queue outside the cinema, ___ we'll have to see another film.
7) I mustn't be late ___ ___ my boss will sack me.
8) Val is a useless secretary; she can ___ type ___ spell properly. ___ her boss is offering her a high salary.

Use of articles

The article

a/an/the

Choosing the right article in English needs very careful consideration. Here are a few general rules to guide you.

1. *a* and *an*
Use *a* before a consonant or a word beginning with U pronounced 'YU':
  a woman, *a* horse, *a* university
Use *an* before a vowel or a word with a silent H: *an* uncle, *an* onion, *an* hour, *an* honest man

2. This is the basic difference between the indefinite article '*a*' and the definite article '*the*':

A (or *an*) is used in *general* statements, for example:
  A gorilla is *a* harmless animal.
This is a statement about all gorillas.
In the plural form of *a*, no article is needed:
  Gorillas are harmless animals.
Similarly, no article is needed with uncountable words:
  Gorillas don't eat meat. (= all meat).

The is used in *particular* statements. For example:
  That's *the* gorilla I saw on television.
This refers to one *special* gorilla. Similarly in the plural:
  I like *the* gorillas in Chessington Zoo.
Here the speaker is referring to certain *particular* gorillas in one *particular* place.

3. Other uses of *a/an*

a) Instead of the number 'one':
  Sally wants to have a dog.
Note that in the *plural* and with *uncountable* words *a* changes to *some*:
  Her mother has *three* dogs/*some* dogs. Here's *some* milk for your dog.

b) With numbers, quantities and measurements:
  100 = *a* hundred   20 = *a* score
  12 = *a* dozen   6 = half *a* dozen
  ½ = *a* half   ¼ = *a* quarter
Note also: *a* lot of/*a* great (good) deal of/*a* great many of
  a large amount of/*a* few/*a* little/quite *a* few, etc.
  30 miles *an* hour/50p *a* kilo/3 times *a* day

c) With certain exclamations:
     What *a* pity! It's *a* shame! That's *a* nuisance!
     What *a* lovely view!

4. Other uses of *the*

a) When there is only *one* of the thing described:
     the Equator, *the* sky, *the* world, *the* Prime Minister

b) Before names of rivers, mountain ranges and seas:
     the Atlantic Ocean, *the* river Thames

c) With superlatives:
     the most expensive, *the* best, *the* biggest

d) With rooms or objects in the house when only one thing could possibly be referred to:
     She's in *the* kitchen. Could you pass me *the* salt please.
     Where's *the* bottle-opener? (but: Can I have *a* knife?)

5. Note how *the* is used or omitted in the sentences below:
     Bert is a burglar. He is *in prison.*
     His wife is going *to the prison* to visit him.
     It's Sunday; Mrs Rose has gone *to church.*
     It's Monday; the tourists have gone *to the church* to take photos.
     He's ill; he must go *to hospital.*
     The doctor goes *to the hospital* at ten o'clock every morning.

The article is omitted when the place referred to (prison, church, hospital) is being used by the subject for its main purpose (for locking up criminals, for religion, for caring for sick people).

6. Idiomatic expressions
     to tell *a* story/*a* joke/*a* lie
     but: to tell *the* truth/speak *the* truth

7. Changing from *a* to *the*

Remember that if you mention something a second time you must change 'a' to 'the'. For example:
     She saw *a* lovely parrot in a cage, but when she tried to stroke it, *the* parrot bit her.
     He watched *a* man go into a jeweller's shop; a little later *the* man came running out with a gun.
The reason for this is that the parrot and the man have already been mentioned. This makes them special.

88

8. *other/others/another/the others/the other*

another = a second, third or an extra (use it only with a countable word in the singular):

> Would you like *another* cake? (but – *some* more wine)
> The film director needs *another* actor. (= one more)

other/others in contrast with *some*:

> *Some* people wore suits; *others* (= other people) wore jeans.
>   (general statement)

the other/the others:

> Twenty people were killed in the plane crash; *the others* were injured.
> Half the audience applauded the play; *the other* half left the theatre.
>   (refers to a particular number of people)

9. Omission of the article

We have already noted that an uncountable word does not need an article when used in a general sense:

> Gorillas dislike meat.

The same is true of *abstract* nouns:

> Gorillas dislike *noise*.
> He's interested in *politics*.

Other examples:

a) With names of people, countries, mountains, towns, titles, institutions:
>   He's taken some photos of Alice, Scotland, Mount Snowdon, Aberdeen, Prince Charles, and Edinburgh University.

b) With names of materials:
>   These shoes are made of leather.

c) With days, months and festivals:
>   I saw him on Tuesday/in December/after Christmas.

d) With sports:
>   He enjoys playing tennis. (but – A game of tennis)

Note that *the* is used with a musical instrument:
> She plays *the* piano/*the* guitar.

EXERCISE 83

Complete these pairs of sentences with a word (*the, a, an, another*, etc) in place of the dash (＿) if it is needed, otherwise cross out the dash.

1) ＿ Mary likes ＿ pop music./She can't stand ＿ music of ＿ Mozart.
2) ＿ honest person tells ＿ truth./ ＿ boy in ＿ classroom told ＿ lie.
3) Johnny has gone to ＿ school./At 4 pm his mother is going to ＿ school to collect him.
4) This fork is dirty; can I have ＿ one./Some of ＿ children are working, ＿ ＿ are in ＿ playground.

5) Is Jim playing ____ football on ____ football pitch?/No he's
playing ____ violin in ____ lounge.
6) He went for ____ swim and found ____ beautiful stone at ____ bottom
of ____ sea./But when he took ____ stone out of ____ water, it lost its colour
and he threw ____ stone back.

EXERCISE 84

Read the following passage and replace each dash (____) with *a/an,/* or *the.* As in
the last exercise, in some cases no word is required.
Description of St. Ives
St. Ives is ____ beautiful old fishing-port on ____ north coast of Cornwall. It is
built on ____ slope round ____ picturesque bay. ____ houses are jumbled
together and ____ streets are narrow. ____ cars have to be parked
in ____ carparks at ____ top of ____ hill.
____ town is rich in ____ history. There is ____ legend that ____ St Ia came
to ____ Cornwall from ____ Ireland in ____ fifth century in ____ tiny boat
(____ Irish say on ____ leaf!). He built ____ fortress on ____ island (which in
true Irish fashion is now no longer ____ island but joined to ____ mainland
by ____ sand,) and ____ town took his name. By ____ Middle Ages, ____ name
St Ia had changed to St Ives. It was developed as ____ fishing-port and became
famous for ____ pilchards. ____ look-out man used to call out ____ fishermen
when he saw ____ shoal of ____ fish. But by ____ end of ____ last
century, ____ fish had moved to ____ other waters.
At ____ same time, with ____ opening of ____ railway in ____ 1880s, ____
artists started moving into ____ fishermen's cottages. One of ____ most famous
was Whistler and ____ other was Sickert. They found that ____ light suited
them because it had ____ high ultraviolet content.
____ town is still popular with ____ artists and has ____ great many attractions
including ____ famous Leach Pottery and ____ only Museum of
Cinematography in ____ Britain. To ____ east of ____ town there
is ____ wonderful Birds' Paradise and ____ Children's Zoo. ____ Model Village
nearby has ____ lot of ____ attractions including ____ Museum
of ____ Smuggling. Unfortunately, ____ town is crowded with ____ tourists
in ____ July and ____ August but it is still worth ____ visit. ____ inhabitants are
particularly proud to have given ____ home to Barbara Hepworth, ____ most
famous artist of ____ century, and now regard their town as ____ San Francisco
of ____ England.

'Difficult' verbs

The student of English occasionally has difficulty in understanding how to use certain verbs or verb formations, some of which he hears repeatedly. The following notes should help you overcome some of these problems.

Common verbs

1. *Make/do*
These rules will help you to decide which of these two verbs to choose:
a) *do* + a job/an activity
>   *do* the shopping, *do* some work
b) *make* + an object (using your hands)
>   *make* a cake, *make* a model plane
c) *make* + an action following a process of thought
>   *make* a decision/a choice/an offer/an
>   announcement/a promise/an excuse
Note the idiom '*make up* your mind': it means you *decide* upon something.

Some phrases which don't fit into these categories are:
>   *make* war/*do* a favour/*do* your best.

EXERCISE 85

Look at this sentence:
>   Mrs Burns has to do a lot of housework today.
Write down her chores from the list below using *do* or *make*: *Mrs Burns has to . . .*
  1) the polishing
  2) an apple pie
  3) a shopping-list
  4) some sewing
  5) the ironing
  6) an omelette
  7) the washing-up
  8) a sweater
  9) home-made jam
 10) some spring-cleaning

2. *Get*
This is perhaps the most common verb in English and can often be replaced with a better verb.
a) *get* = reach/arrive at
>   He *got* to the station late.
b) *have got* = possess/own
>   He *has got* two cars.

c) *have got to* = must (see page 62)
d) *get* = earn
  He *gets* £500 a month.
e) *get* = become/grow
  Children *get* taller every day. He's *getting* fat.
  David is *getting* tired/angry/hot/worried/bored/hungry.

Sometimes, usually where the change is to something bad or unpleasant, *go* is used instead of *get*:
(of the body) *go* blind/deaf/mad/red (blush)/pale (illness)/bald
(of things) Milk *goes* sour./Milk *goes* off/bad.

EXERCISE 86

Make sentences choosing a phrase from List A to go with one from List B:

	A		B
	1) go red		a) get sick.
	2) tremble		b) get excited.
Children	3) cry	when they	c) get angry.
	4) scream		d) get frightened.
	5) go pale		e) get upset.
	6) go wild		f) get embarrassed.

3. *Keep/kept*

a) *keep* = to have something in a particular place over a period of time
  He *keeps* his bike in the garage.
  She *keeps* rabbits in her garden.
b) *keep* + gerund(*-ing*) = to do something frequently/all the time
  Note that this form is often used in making criticisms:
  The waiter *keeps dropping* plates.
  I *keep losing* my pen.
c) *keep* + adjective = continue in this state
  You must *keep* awake/still/quiet.

4. *Catch/caught*

a) *catch* a ball (= take it in your hands after someone has thrown it to you)
b) *catch* a fish (= bring it out of the water on a fishing line)
c) *catch* a bus (= to get on a bus)
d) *catch* a cold (= become ill with a cold)

5. *Miss*

a) *miss* a bus (= fail to catch it because you were late)
b) *miss* my family (= feel unhappy because my family aren't with me)

Phrasal verbs

A *phrasal verb* is made up of a verb and a preposition – for example, *turn on*:

> He asked me to *turn on* the television.

With *most* of these phrasal verbs the object ('television' in this example) may go before or after the preposition:

> He asked me to *turn* the television *on*.

But if the object is a pronoun, it goes before the preposition:

> He asked me to turn *it* on.

There are many of these verbs in English and the common words *come, go, break, put*, etc can produce at least ten new verbs with different meanings.

In some cases, the preposition alters the meaning of several verbs in the same way. Here are some of the most important examples.

1. *Up* can show that an action is done and completed over a period of time

> *Drink up* your milk.(= drink all of it)
> I've *used up* all the stamps. (= used all of them)

Other verbs like this are *eat up/wash up/dry up/tidy up/clean up/clear up/save up* (= save an amount of money)

2. *Up* can show completion of a task involving the hands

Some verbs like this are *wrap up/fold up/roll up/do up/tie up/button up/zip up/lock up*:

> They *rolled up* the carpet and carried it out.

The negative forms of these verbs are made by putting *un-* in front of the verb instead of *up* after it:

> Children *unwrap* their Christmas presents on December 25th.
> He *untied* his shoelaces and took them off.

EXERCISE 87

Write out these sentences choosing one of the verbs above:
1) It's cold; ___ ___ your coat.
2) After lunch the waitresses have to ___ ___ the table-cloths.
3) I can't clean my teeth; someone has ___ ___ all the toothpaste.
4) Johnny wants to ___ his birthday present but he can't ___ the knot.
5) If you want to dance you'll have to ___ ___ the carpets.
6) ___ ___ your icecream, we must hurry.
7) Her husband always ___ ___ the dishes and then she ___ them ___ with a tea-towel.
8) He's ___ ___ to buy a new motor-bike.
9) We must ___ ___ the house before the guests arrive.

3. *Up* can show violence. This is common in conversation.

Some verbs like this are *smash up/break up/beat up/tear up/rip up*:

> He's *smashed up* his new car. (= seriously damaged it)
> She *tore up* her boyfriend's letters. (= tore them into pieces)

4. *Down* can show destruction
Some verbs like this are *cut down* (trees)/*pull down* (old buildings)/*tear down* (posters)/*knock down* (someone on a road)/*fall down* (= collapse):
> The lorry *knocked down* a pedestrian.

5. *Down* can show that something is written on paper
Some verbs like this are *write down*/*take down*/*jot down*/*scribble down*/*copy down*:
> During the meeting, the secretary *took down* some notes.

6. *On* can show that something continues
Some verbs like this are *walk on*/*drive on*/*keep on*/*fly on*/*go on*:
> They stopped at a roadside cafe and then *drove on* for another hour.

Note that *go on* often means 'go on talking'
> The speaker *went on and on* and no one could interrupt him.

7. *On* can show an idea of connection
Some of the verbs like this are *put on*/*stick on*/*pin on*/*tie on*/*fasten on*/*sew on*:
> He asked his mother *to sew* a badge *on* his jacket.

Note that *turn on* and *switch on* can mean 'start working':
> It's getting dark; *turn* the light *on*.

EXERCISE 88   Choose a phrasal verb to say how you would
1) start a tape-recorder.
2) put a stamp on an envelope.
3) put a notice on the notice-board.
4) put on a medal.
5) put a blackboard on the wall. (using a hammer)
6) put a button on a shirt.

8. *Off* can show the idea of leaving a fixed place
Jim is sitting on a wall. He may leave it in several ways:
> He can *get off* or *jump off*.
> He can *fall off*. (by mistake)
> Someone may *push*/*knock*/*pull* him *off*. (force him to leave)

EXERCISE 89   Choose a suitable verb with *off* for each of these sentences:
1) A bus hit the cyclist and ___ him ___ his bicycle.
2) She ___ the cat ___ the armchair.
3) It was so hot that he ___ ___ his jacket.
4) The cowboy ___ ___ his horse and went into the bar.
5) A Red Indian hit him with an arrow and he ___ ___ his horse.
6) The notice in the park said: ' ___ ___ the grass'.

9. *Off* can show the idea of moving away
Some verbs like this are *go off*/*run off*/*drive off*/*rush off*/*walk off*/*hurry off*.
These three verbs are useful to remember:
> The referee *sent off* the player. (= he told him to leave the pitch for bad behaviour)

The aeroplane *took off* at five o'clock. (= left the ground)
Someone has *walked off with* my pen. (= someone has taken or
stolen it)

EXERCISE 90

Complete these sentences.
1) He got into his car and ___ ___ .
2) The thief grabbed her handbag and ___ ___ .
3) He ___ the dogs ___ the flowers in his garden.
4) That player is too rough; the referee should ___ ___ ___ .
5) He looked at his watch, gave a cry and ___ ___ .
6) The plane ___ ___ from Gatwick airport at 7 am.

Answer the questions in Exercises 91, 92 and 93 by forming a phrasal verb from one of the nine types just listed, and using one of the following verbs (some may be used twice):

cut/knock/drink/write/drive/tear/save/eat/sew/wrap/
take/stick/lock/tie/clear/wipe/fold

EXERCISE 91

What must you do in each of these situations?
1) A button has come off your shirt. (Answer: I must ___ it ___ .)
2) There's some dust on one of your records.
3) You're going away and you're afraid your house may be robbed.
4) You want £1000 in your bank by the end of the year.
5) Your small child wants some meat – he can't use a knife.
6) You must send off a parcel using (a) brown paper (b) string (c) a label for the address.
7) Someone tells you his phone number – you have a bad memory.
8) You've finished reading your newspaper.

EXERCISE 92

What do the following do?
1) lumberjacks. (Answer: They ___ ___ trees.)
2) demolition men.
3) planes when they start on a journey.
4) a bus waiting at a bus-stop when the conductor rings the bell.
5) a secretary at a business meeting.

EXERCISE 93

There is a large dog in the dining-room. What do you think has happened?
1) John's dinner has disappeared.
2) His glass of milk is empty.
3) A vase of flowers is on the floor.
4) The newspaper is in tiny pieces.
5) What must John do when he finds the mess?

Adjectives and adverbs

Adjectives

Adjectives describe people or things. They go *before* or *after* the noun, and *after* forms of the verbs be/seem/feel/taste/look.

When there is more than one adjective, the most *general* adjective comes first. Look at these three sentences:

> She wore a lovely green dress.
> It was a dark, cold night.
> He looked tired and hungry.

In the first sentence, there is no comma (,) or 'and' between the two adjectives 'lovely' and 'green'. This is because 'lovely' is a *general* adjective (like 'nice', 'good', 'bad', etc), whereas 'green' is *specific* (because it is the name of a particular colour). So the two kinds of adjective combine to give one picture of the dress. In the second sentence, both the adjectives ('dark' and 'cold') are *specific*, and each says a different thing about the night. They are therefore separated by a comma. The third sentence shows how two adjectives *after a verb* are joined by 'and'.

Most adjectives can be learnt from your dictionary but a few need special care. Here is a list of some of these with their opposites:

generous (giving freely)	mean
lovely (very nice)	awful
enjoyable (very pleasant)	boring
calm (the sea)	rough
smooth (skin)	rough
gentle (behaviour)	rough
soft (material)	hard
tough (strong)	weak
tender (meat)	tough
harmful (having a bad effect)	harmless

Some adjectives have alternatives for giving special emphasis. Mice are *small*: ants are *tiny*; fleas are *minute*.

big	huge	enormous
nice	lovely	wonderful
cross	angry	furious
attractive	pretty	beautiful (girl)
slim	thin	skinny

EXERCISE 94

Choose the best word from the lists above:
1) Boxers must be ___ .
2) He felt sea-sick because the sea was so ___ .
3) Many doctors believe smoking is ___ .
4) I can't cut this meat; it's too ___ .
5) Receiving £20,000 was a ___ surprise.
6) The film was so ___ that he fell asleep.
7) It was an ___ party and they left after ten minutes.
8) Silk feels ___ .
9) Brazil is a ___ country; Malta is a ___ island.
10) He's so ___ that he never offers anyone a cigarette.

Further practice
Read the following passage and answer the questions below. You may find it helpful to use your dictionary.

National characteristics
Is there such a thing as a national character? Is it true, for example, to say that Italians are *lively*, Spaniards are *proud*, Germans are *serious* or Americans are *noisy*? In every country there are *stupid* people and *intelligent* people, *aggressive* people and *peaceful* people and, of course, *selfish* people and *kind* people. Perhaps it is *ridiculous* to speak about a whole country; people are individuals, not types. However, most people who travel feel that other people have certain common qualities and this leads to phrases like: 'He is typically English' or 'typically French'. Often these opinions are based on history. They are old-fashioned and were perhaps never true even in the past.

What about the people in Britain? Here are some common opinions – see if you agree with them.

> *The English*: they don't like to speak about their private life or to show exactly what they are feeling. They often dress or behave strangely.

> *The Scots*: they like to save their money and don't spend it on things which they don't really need. They have provided the world's greatest explorers and have also been responsible for many important inventions. They don't like to make quick decisions.

> *The Welsh*: they are usually dark-haired and tend to get excited or angry very easily. They love singing and poetry. They don't trust strangers.

> *The Irish*: They talk a lot and often have a very nice manner. They tend to live in the clouds and sometimes behave in a totally irrational or crazy way.

EXERCISE 95

1) Find the opposites of these words in the passage:
   a) dull   b) quiet   c) modest   d) sensible   e) modern
2) Which of the four British nationalities is described as being:
   musical   adventurous   talkative   dreamy   eccentric   charming
   excitable   suspicious   reserved   cautious?
3) Are the Scots thrifty or extravagant? Are they inventive?
4) In what way are the Irish the opposite of the English?

Formation of adjectives

Many adjectives are formed by adding -y to a noun (thrift/thrifty) or by changing final -e to -y: (noise/noisy). Here are ten examples, all relating to weather:

> icy   windy   chilly   rainy   misty   foggy
> stormy   sunny   frosty   cloudy

EXERCISE 96

Select the best word for each space in the following passage:

Many visitors think the British weather is so ____ that they need an umbrella every day. Of course the sky is often dark and ____ and it can be quite ____ too, though there are never hurricanes, as there are in America. At times the North Sea is so ____ that it is dangerous for fishermen. Some tourists who have read Sherlock Holmes stories believe that London is always ____ and that they will easily get lost. This is not true, though occasionally it is ____ by the river early in the morning. The hottest period, with nice ____ days, should be July and August, while the most ____ is always January, when the ground is usually ____ in the morning and the roads are slippery because they are so ____ .

The past participle or -ed ending

Past participles are often used as adjectives:
> a *frightened* mouse   a *broken* cup

This is very common in describing people:
> The farmer has a red face.   He is a *red-faced* farmer.
> Sue has blue eyes.   She is a *blue-eyed* girl.

You must use a hyphen (-) to show that it is the farmer's face which is red, not the farmer.

EXERCISE 97

Change these sentences as in the example

> George *has* dark hair, no moustache, and wears dirty old jeans.
> George *is* dark-haired, clean-shaven and badly-dressed.

1) Jane has fair hair, blue eyes, and is wearing a smart dress.
2) Fred has short hair and a bad temper.
3) Fred's father has a kind heart but dislikes anything modern.
4) His trousers had creases and his shoes hadn't been polished.
5) The toast was black and the coffee didn't have any sugar in it.
6) The athlete has a strong will but a big head. (= he is proud)

Self

The word 'selfish' means thinking of your own interests and not caring about other people.

The form *self-* is placed before certain adjectives (or nouns) to show that the word refers to the subject.

> To be *self-confident* is to be confident in yourself.
> To be *self-pitying* is to feel sorry for yourself.
> To be *self-controlled* is to have control over your own feelings.

EXERCISE 98

Choose a word from the list below to complete the sentences:

self-confident   self-critical   self-centred (= very selfish)   self-service
self-made   self-conscious   self-winding   self-satisfied

1) He's too ___ to understand Pat's problems.
2) He always blushes because he is so ___ .
3) He spoke of his success in a ___ way.
4) The artist was very ___ and always thought his work could be better.
5) This rich businessman started from nothing; he is a ___ man.
6) He's very ___ and thinks he will be Prime Minister.
7) This is a ___ watch; you don't have to touch it.
8) This is a ___ restaurant.

Over/under

Look at these sentences:

> Those bananas are yellow. They are ready to eat. They are *ripe*.
> These bananas are black. They are old. They are *over-ripe*.
> These bananas are green. They are not ready to eat. They are *under-ripe*.

Over- gives the idea *too much* while *under-* gives the idea *not enough*. Note that the hyphen may be omitted and the words joined: underripe.

Read the following passage and then answer the questions in Exercise 99:

Report from the Hotel and Restaurant Association
After inspecting the premises of ——'s Restaurant, we feel it is impossible to recommend it as a member of our organisation. There were not nearly enough waiters for a restaurant of its size and the waiters we saw looked worn out with rushing about. We understand that the waiters receive a very low salary and they all looked very thin and more in need of a meal than the customers! We also thought that the tables and chairs were much too close together for comfort and the food was unsatisfactory – the potatoes were hard and the steak was too tough to cut. The grapes we had for dessert tasted very bitter. Then we found that the bill was more than it should have been. The room was far too hot and we were glad to get out in the fresh air again. We had heard that this was a wonderful restaurant but it had obviously been regarded too highly.

EXERCISE 99

Answer these questions choosing one of the following words, joined with *under* or *over*. (Example: paid = He was overpaid.)

> paid   heated   crowded   staffed   fed   worked
> charged   ripe   done   cooked

1) There weren't enough waiters, so the restaurant was ___ .
2) The waiters were tired because they were ___ .
3) They didn't receive a good salary. They were ___ .
4) They were very thin because they were ___ .
5) There were too many chairs and tables, so the restaurant was ___ .
6) What was wrong with the potatoes? ___ ___ ___ .
7) Why do you think the steak was so tough? ___ ___ ___ .
8) Were the grapes ready to eat? No, they were ___ .
9) The inspector was angry about his bill because he was ___ .
10) It was hot because the room was ___ .
11) Do you think the restaurant had been overrated or underrated? ___ ___ ___ ___ .

Describing things

Compare these sentences:

>Charlie Chaplin films are *amusing*. (= funny)
>People are *amused* by Charlie Chaplin films. (= they laugh or smile)

In the first example, the adjective describes a thing (films).
But the *-ing* ending may also describe a person as he seems to other people:

>Charlie Chaplin is an *amusing* comedian. (= he makes other people laugh)

Here are some examples of the most common forms – those in columns B and C are stronger or more emphatic.

A	B	C
frightening	terrifying	appalling
annoying	infuriating	maddening
interesting	exciting	thrilling
uninteresting	boring	deadly
worrying	disturbing	alarming
touching	moving	heartrending
confusing	puzzling	bewildering
surprising	amazing *or* astonishing (= very surprising)	astounding *or* staggering (= extremely surprising)
upsetting (= unpleasantly surprising)	shocking	horrifying

EXERCISE 100

Choose one of the words above which you think could describe these different types of films:

1) a film with a lot of action
2) a comedy which makes you smile
3) a film which makes you scream
4) a film which shows a lot of blood
5) a film which you can't understand
6) a documentary film about building roads
7) a film which makes you cry
8) a film about ghosts and vampires

How would you describe these situations?

9) The telephone wakes you up at 2 am in the morning
10) a mathematical problem you can't solve
11) a telegram tells you that you have won £50,000 in a lottery
12) the sight of injured people after a car-crash
13) your suitcases have got lost at the airport
14) your child hasn't come home and it's late
15) a bank-robber points a gun at you

Describing feelings

Use the *past* tense forms of all the words in the list on the previous page –
exciting → *excited*/worrying → *worried*, etc – to help you show how you or other
people feel.

Here are a few more very common words which are important:

cheerful (in a good mood)	depressed (in a bad mood)
pleased	upset (sad because of bad news)
flattered	hurt (sad because offended)
innocent	guilty
embarrassed	relaxed
shy	confident
ashamed	proud
timid/afraid/scared	
(words of fear)	

These words may follow the verb 'be' or 'feel'. The meaning is the same:
He is *embarrassed* = He feels *embarrassed*.

EXERCISE 101
Choose a word from the list above to complete these sentences:
1) Marion was ___ when John criticised her hair-style.
2) Marion was ___ when her cat died.
3) Marion was ___ when I admired her painting.
4) Marion was ___ when she saw a spider.
5) Marion was ___ when her boyfriend saw her with another boy.
6) Marion was ___ when she realised she had forgotten her mother's birthday.
7) The miserable weather made her feel ___ .
8) People whistle when they are ___ .
9) Squirrels are ___ .
10) The child was too ___ to speak.

Adverbs of manner

Look at these sentences:
      a) Susan is a careful driver.   She drives *carefully*.
      b) She always looks tidy.   She dresses *tidily*.
      c) She is a sensible person.   She behaves *sensibly*.
      d) She is a good tennis player.   She plays tennis *well*.
      e) She is a fast runner.   She runs *fast*.
The words in *italics* are called adverbs of manner. They describe verbs and tell us
how (that is, in what *manner*) Susan drives, dresses, etc.

Each of the sentences shows you how to form a different kind of adverb of manner. With most adjectives, you simply add -*ly* (see sentence a). The -*y* ending on an adjective changes to -*ily* (see sentence b). The -*le* ending changes to -*ly* (sentence c). Sentence d) shows that the adverb form of 'good is 'well'. You will see from sentence e) that some adjectives remain unchanged in their adverb form.

When do you use adverbs of manner?

Use adverbs of manner to describe a verb, as in the examples above, or before an adjective or another adverb:

> He's *terribly* kind. He drove *dangerously* fast.

What position do these adverbs have in the sentence?

a) They usually follow the verb, as in the examples above.

b) They never come between verb and object:

> 'She plays tennis *well*', **not** '*well* tennis'.

c) They can go before the verb for special emphasis:

> When he saw his teacher, he *quickly* hid the cigarette.

d) Words like *suddenly/luckily* often go at the beginning for dramatic effect:

> There was a plane crash. *Luckily/Amazingly*, no one was hurt.

Note that you should use an adjective, not an adverb, after the verbs be, look, seem, sound, feel, taste

> He is *rich*. You look *awful*. This tastes *nice*.

EXERCISE 102

Change these sentences using an adverb as in this example:

She is a *bad opera singer*.	*She sings opera badly*.
1) That dog sounds angry.	It's barking ___ .
2) The soldiers are brave.	They're fighting ___ .
3) Pigs are greedy.	They eat ___ .
4) Her dentist is gentle.	He treats his patients ___ .
5) The moon is bright.	It's shining ___ .
6) She's a good actress.	She acts ___ .
7) It's a slow train.	The train is going ___ .
8) The politician was sincere.	He spoke ___ .
9) He's a bad comedian.	He tells jokes ___ .
10) He's a wonderful painter.	He paints ___ .

EXERCISE 103

Choose the best adverb from the list on the right and complete the sentences, beginning each one with He . . . or She . . .

1) shouted	hard
2) stroked the cat	distinctly
3) ate a huge chicken	carefully
4) crept upstairs	gently
5) yawned	angrily
6) spoke on the phone	clumsily
7) bolted the door	greedily
8) packed the china cups	securely
9) dropped the vase	slowly
10) worked	wearily

Common conversational phrases

Here are some common phrases which it is very important to learn, as they are always used in polite conversation.

1. *Would you like* . . .? This is used when making an offer.

Would you like some coffee? Yes please. I'm thirsty.
Would you like a cigarette? No thanks. I don't smoke.
Would you like a cake? No thanks. I'm not hungry.
Would you like an aspirin? Yes please. I've got a headache.

EXERCISE 104

Now complete the sentences below:
1) Would you ____ some milk? No thanks. I'm not ____ .
2) ____ you ____ a biscuit? Yes please.
3) Would ____ ____ some toast? No thanks. I'm ____ ____ .
4) ____ ____ ____ a chocolate? ____ ____ . I've got toothache.
5) ____ ____ ____ a fire in your room? No ____ . I don't feel ____ .

2. *Would you like to* . . .? This is used when making an invitation.

Would you like to dance? Yes, I'd love to.
Would you like to come to my party tomorrow? *I'm afraid* I can't; I must study for my exams.

The phrase *I'm afraid* is the polite form for refusing an invitation.
Notice how *I'm afraid* is used in this situation. Fred has just met a very pretty girl called Mary. He wants to invite her out and get to know her. Unfortunately, she already has a boyfriend and can't go out with Fred.

EXERCISE 105

Look at Fred's invitations in questions 1–5 below and choose the best excuse from her answers (a–e).

1) Would you like to go to a café?
2) Would you like to go swimming?
3) Would you like to go to the cinema tomorrow?
4) Would you like to hear my guitar?
5) Would you like to come out with me next week?

a) I'm afraid I've got a cold.
b) I'm afraid I must wash my hair.
c) I'm afraid I'm not hungry.
d) I'm afraid I'll be very busy.
e) I'm afraid I've got a headache.

3. *I'd rather* . . . . This is used for showing a preference.

> Would you like to play cards? No thanks. *I'd rather* play football.
> Would you like some wine? No thanks. *I'd rather* have a glass of water.

Where there is no question, *I'd rather* must be followed by the word *than*.

> *I'd rather* go to a pub *than* stay at home.
> *I'd rather* have fish *than* meat.

I'd sooner has exactly the same meaning and is used in the same way.

> *I'd sooner* go to a pub *than* stay at home.

EXERCISE 106

Complete the sentences:

1) Would you like a sandwich?
   No thanks. I'm ＿＿ hungry. I'd ＿＿ have a cigarette.
2) ＿＿ ＿＿ ＿＿ a lift in my car?
   No ＿＿ . I'm ＿＿ tired. I'd ＿＿ walk.
3) ＿＿ ＿＿ ＿＿ a glass of milk?
   No ＿＿ . I'm ＿＿ thirsty. I'd ＿＿ ＿＿ a chocolate.
4) I'd ＿＿ work on a farm ＿＿ in an office.
5) What ＿＿ ＿＿ ＿＿ do, have a picnic or go to a restaurant?
   I'd ＿＿ ＿＿ a picnic.

4. *Shall I* . . .? This is used when offering to do something for another person.

> *Shall I* carry your suitcase for you? Thank you. That's very kind of you
> *Shall I* help you with those dishes? No, don't worry; I can manage.

Imagine that Mr Burns is an elderly patient in hospital. He can't get out of bed.
His nurse is very nice and wants to help him.

Mr Burns	This room is freezing. It must be 5°C.
Nurse:	Shall I turn on the heater?
Mr Burns:	I'm very thirsty.
Nurse:	Shall I get you some more water?

EXERCISE 107

Now imagine that *you* are the nurse – what will you say?

1) *Mr Burns*: It's terribly draughty. That window is open.
2) *Mr Burns*: I'm really hungry.
3) *Mr Burns*: I think it's time for my favourite programme on TV.
4) (The phone rings.) *Mr Burns*: Oh, who on earth can that be?
5) (Mr Burns yawns.) *Mr Burns*: I'd better get some sleep.

5. *Could you, can you, would you mind* . . . ? These forms are used when you want
someone to help you, or do something for you, or give you some information.

> *Can you* pass me that ashtray, please? Yes, of course.
> *Could you* post this letter for me, please? Yes, of course.
> Excuse me – *can you* tell me the way to Oxford Street, please? I'm
> afraid not; I'm a stranger in London myself.

EXERCISE 108
Now look back at the scene in the hospital and imagine you are Mr Burns. Using the clues, ask the nurse to do some things for you. For example:
    (cold) Can you turn on the heater, please?
    (thirsty) Could you get me a drink please?
1) draughty
2) hungry   4) phone
3) TV   5) tired

Use *would you mind* when speaking to someone you don't know. Remember that it is always followed by a verb in the gerund form.
    Would you mind waiting outside, please?
    Would you mind closing the door?
Note that *would you mind* is also often used when someone is annoying you. For example, you are trying to study, but some students next to you are talking a lot.
    Would you mind making less noise?
One of them is listening to a radio. You might say:
    Would you mind turning that radio off?

EXERCISE 109
Imagine that you are talking to a complete stranger. Ask him to:
1) show you the way to the Post Office
2) take your aunt to hospital
3) help you carry a suitcase
4) smoke outside
5) change your table-cloth for a clean one

May I, can I, do you mind if . . .? These forms are used when you are asking permission to do something.

Imagine that Johnny is a little boy having tea with his grandmother: he feels hungry.
Johnny: *May I* have a sandwich, please?
Grandmother: Yes, help yourself.
Johnny: *Can I* have a biscuit please?
Grandmother: Yes, of course.
Johnny: *May I* have another cake, please?
Grandmother: No, I think you've had enough.
Now Johnny feels thirsty.
Johnny: Please *can I* have some Coca-Cola?
Grandmother: *Yes, all right.* Here you are.

EXERCISE 110
1) Now Johnny wants to leave the table. Write down what you think he says.
2) He also wants to watch TV. . .
3) to play in the garden
4) to go upstairs
5) to take the dog for a walk.

Use the form *do you mind if . . . ?* when making a more important request:

> *Do you mind* if I use your phone?
>
> *Do you mind if* I bring my sister to your party?

6. *Shall we . . . , let's (let us) . . . , what about* or *how about* + gerund

These are used for making suggestions involving yourself and another person (or other people):

> *Shall we* play tennis? Yes, that would be lovely.
>
> *Shall we* dance? Yes, all right.

Use *let's* when you very much want to do the thing you are suggesting:

> *Let's* have a party! That's a good idea.
>
> *Let's* all go to the circus!

There is also a negative form with *not*:

> *Let's not* do any more work = Shall we stop working?

The form *what about . . .* is a suggestion offered to another person either to help him or to invite his opinion.

> 'I can't get my car to start.'
>
> '*What about* asking Ted to look at it; he's a mechanic.'
>
> 'That's a good idea. I didn't think of that.'

> 'I don't want to see this film.'
>
> *What about* going to another cinema?'
>
> 'No, it's too late now.'

EXERCISE 111

Here are two dialogues between two friends on holiday. Replace the words in *italics* with a phrase from the list below:

1) A: Shall we *have a swim*?

   B: No, it's too cold.

   A: Then what about *going fishing*?

   B: That's a good idea. Let's do that.

   go water-skiing; playing basket-ball; go surfing; having a picnic; have an icecream; going to a café; lie down on the sand; going for a run

2) A: shall we *go to the casino*?

   B: No, it's too expensive.

   A: Then let's *have a game of tennis*.

   have some champagne; have a glass of beer; go by taxi; walk; buy some caviar; buy some sardines; stay at a first-class hotel; stay in a caravan

7. *What's the matter (with), What's wrong (with) . . . ?*

These are used when a person seems to be ill or suffering.

> *What's the matter with* Jane? She won't talk to anyone.

It's more usual to use *what's wrong* when referring to things.

> *What's wrong with* the television? There's no picture.

When you are speaking to someone directly, the 'with' must be omitted, e.g.:

> 'What's the matter with Jane?'
>
> *but* 'What's the matter, Jane?'

EXERCISE 112

Complete these pictures.
1) ___ the matter with George? He's got a toothache.
2) What's ___ ___ ___ bike? It's got a puncture.
3) ___ ___ ___ ___ the boss? He's lost his temper.
4) What's ___ ___ ___ you? I've got a cold.
5) ___ ___ ___ your radio? It's got no batteries.

Notice the forms *It doesn't matter, Never mind. . . .*
These are polite forms which you can use after someone says sorry to you.

        A) Excuse me, can I have some wine please?
        B) Yes, of course. Help yourself.
        A) Thanks a lot. Oh, I'm sorry. I've spilt some on your carpet.
        B) *It doesn't matter.*

        A) Excuse me, can I borrow your lighter, please?
        B) Yes, here you are.
        A) Oh dear! I'm afraid that I've broken it.
        B) *Never mind,* I have another one.

EXERCISE 113

Look at the conversation below and complete the empty spaces with one of the conversational phrases that you have just learnt.
Lady Ascot has just entered a high-class restaurant.

Waiter: ___ ___ take your coat?
Lady Ascot: No, thank you. It's cold here. ___ ___ keep it on.
Waiter: ___ ___ ___ ___ sit here?
Lady Ascot: No. Do you ___ ___ I sit over there by the window?
Waiter: No, of course not. Come this way please.
(A minute later)
Lady Ascot: Waiter! ___ ___ ___ the menu please?
Waiter: Yes, of ___ . Here you are. What ___ ___ ___ ___ start with?
Lady Ascot: Let me think . . . Yes ___ ___ some soup, please.
Waiter: I'm ___ , I don't understand. Do you want to wash your hands?
Lady Ascot: No, I didn't ask for soap. I said I want some soup.
           Would ___ ___ bringing me some hot mushroom soup, please.
(Five minutes later)
Waiter: Here you are, Madam. ___ ___ ___ anything else?
Lady Ascot: Yes, ___ ___ ___ a roll and butter, and also some pepper please.
Waiter: Paper? What do you want paper for, Madam?
Lady Ascot: Are you deaf or something? I said I wanted some pepper and, waiter, ___ ___ ___ changing this soup, I can't bear it when it's cold.
Waiter: I'm very ___ . ___ ___ get you some salt, too?
(Half an hour later)
Lady Ascot: ___ ___ , ___ ___ ___ the bill please, I'm in rather a hurry.
Waiter: Yes, of course. Here you are, Madam.

Lady Ascot:	Oh dear! This is terrible.
Waiter:	Why, what's the matter, Madam?
Lady Ascot:	___ ___ I've forgotten to bring my purse and I haven't any money on me. ___ ___ ___ if I come in and pay you tomorrow morning?
Waiter:	No, ___ ___ the manager would never agree to that. ___ ___ ___ coming with me to the kitchen and putting on this apron. ___ ___ you'll have to help me do the washing-up.

EXERCISE 114

Answer the questions below after you have completed the dialogue.

1) What does the waiter offer to do when the lady enters the restaurant?
2) Why does the lady say she'd rather keep her coat on?
3) Where does the lady wish to sit?
4) What is the first thing the lady asks for?
5) What kind of soup does she ask for?
6) Why does she ask the waiter to change her soup?
7) Why can't she pay her bill?
8) What does the waiter make her do?

Here is another conversation. Read it through and pay special attention to the words in *italics*. Then answer the questions. Mrs Burns and Sandra are in a huge department store. They are doing some shopping.

Mrs Burns:	Do we need anything else or *shall we* go home now?
Sandra:	Well, I haven't got any boots for the winter. *What about* going to the shoe department and having a look?
Mrs Burns:	Yes, *let's* do that. Do you know where it is?
Sandra:	No, I don't. Wait a moment, I'll ask someone . . . *Excuse me*, please. *Can you tell me the way to* the shoe department?
Girl:	The ladies' shoe department? Yes, it's upstairs on the first floor.

(In the shoe department)

Shop-assistant:	*Can I* help you, Madam?
Sandra:	Yes, *I'd like* a pair of boots please.
Shop-assistant:	I see. *What kind of* boots would you like? Have you anything particular in mind?
Sandra:	I'm not sure really.
Shop-assistant:	*Would you rather* have real leather or just imitation?
Sandra:	Oh, I'd like real leather.
Shop-assistant:	*What colour* would you like?
Sandra:	Black, please.
Shop-assistant:	These are very nice. *What's your size*, Madam?
Sandra:	I'm not sure. *Can you measure me*, please?
Shop-assistant:	I think you're size 5. *Would you mind trying these on?*
Sandra:	Yes, of course.
Shop-assistant:	How do they feel? Do they *fit* you?

Sandra:	No, *I'm afraid* they're a bit too small. *Could I try on* a larger size please?
Shop-assistant:	Try these; they're size 6.
Sandra:	Oh, these are much better – they fit me perfectly. Do you think they *suit* me, Mummy?
Mrs Burns:	Yes, they look very nice on you and they match your handbag too. But *how much* are they?
Shop-assistant:	£19.99. That's the sale price. I think it's a *bargain*!
Mrs Burns	All right, *We'll take them. Can I* pay by cheque?
Shop-assistant:	Have you got a banker's card?
Mrs Burns:	Yes. Here you are. *May I* have a receipt please?
Shop-assistant:	Yes, of course. *Shall I wrap the boots up* for you?
Mrs Burns:	Yes, if you wouldn't mind. Thanks very much.

EXERCISE 115

The sentences written below are incorrect. Correct them as in the example:

Mrs Burns suggests going to work. *Mrs Burns suggests going home.*

1) Sandra wants to find the coat department.
2) The girl tells her the shoe department is on the ground floor.
3) Sandra wants to buy a pair of shoes.
4) She prefers imitation leather to real leather.
5) She takes size 5.
6) The size 6 boots are uncomfortable.
7) Her mother likes the boots because they are a different colour to her handbag.
8) Mrs Burns wants to pay cash.
9) The assistant thinks the boots are expensive.
10) The assistant offers to tie the boots together.

Question tags

Look at these sentences:

He's the best player on the field, isn't he? Oh, yes.
She can type, can't she? Yes, she's a trained secretary.
She isn't Italian, is she? Well, actually her mother is Italian.

These sentences are not questions, although they always end with a question mark. The endings (isn't he? can't she? is she?) ask the listener to agree or to confirm what is said.

If the listener is unable to agree, it's polite to use the word 'actually':

Susan can drive, *can't she?*

Well, *actually*, she hasn't passed her driving-test yet.

Important:

1) If the main part of the sentence is positive, the verb in the question tag must be negative, with the *n't* ending. Don't use *not* here. If the main part of the sentence is negative, the verb in the question tag must be positive, e.g.:

She can type (*positive*), can't she? (*negative*)
She isn't Italian (*negative*), is she? (*positive*)

2) The question words *do*, *does* and *did* must be used after the simple present and simple past tenses:

> He works hard, *doesn't* he?
> You don't like hamburgers, *do* you?
> He broke the window, *didn't* he?
> They didn't enjoy the party, *did* they?

Sometimes question tags are used to show that the speaker is unsure, worried or nervous, and he wants the listener to calm his fears. This is shown by letting the voice go up at the end of the sentence:

> You're not going to tell the police, *are you?*
> You didn't forget to post that letter, *did you?*
> You won't marry that sailor, *will you?*

When the idea seems obvious (or absurd) you may begin the sentence with '*Surely* . . .' instead of using a question tag:

> *Surely* you're going to give your sister a wedding present!
> *Surely* you're not going to church in a pair of jeans!

Special note:

1) The special verbs *must/should/ought*, etc., change in the same way:

> You should stop smoking, *shouldn't* you?
> You had better hurry, *hadn't* you?

but treat the form 'have to' as a verb:

> Nurses have to work hard, *don't* they?

2) The form 'I am' is followed by 'aren't I?'

3) *Everybody/everyone/nobody/no one*, which are followed by singular verbs, have a plural question tag:

> Everybody enjoyed the party, *didn't they?*
> No one is interested, *are they?*

EXERCISE 116

Choose the correct question tag for the following sentences:

1) Mary is cooking lunch . . .   (*Answer*: . . . isn't she?)
2) We are late . . .
3) It was an amusing film . . .
4) You weren't offended . . .
5) You don't like fish . . .
6) Travelling costs a lot . . .
7) You thought I was mad . . .
8) He didn't wait for me . . .
9) I'm the best boxer here . . .
10) You'll pay me back tomorrow . . .
11) You won't tell anyone this secret . . .
12) You'd better apologise . . .
13) Those children can swim . . .
14) You'd like to be the boss . . .
15) You haven't finished yet . . .
16) Soldiers have to clean their own uniform . . .

17) Everyone admires Jane . . .
18) It's going to snow . . .
19) . . . you're going to see your parents.
20) . . . you're not going to swim in that dirty river!
21) Nobody cares about the future . . .

Telephone conversations

Phoning in English is quite easy but it's important to know a few phrases which are often used.

When answering, first say who you are, or what your number is. If at work, give the name of your office or company. Don't just say 'hello'. If the person has dialled incorrectly say: 'I'm afraid you've got the wrong number.' If the caller asks for *you* say: 'Speaking'.

Look at the meaning of these phrases:

Is John in/there? = is he immediately available?

John is out/has gone out = not immediately available but expected back in a short time.

John is away/has gone away = not expected back for at least a day, maybe longer.

Hold on/hang on/hold the line = wait a little (no more than a minute or two).

Please ring back = telephone again later.

The line is engaged = connected to another caller.

I'll put you through = I'll connect you to the person you want.

I want to reverse the charges = I want the person I'm calling to pay.

I want to make an appointment = I want to fix a time to see a doctor/hairdresser/businessman.

Will that suit you/be convenient for you? = is it a good time or a suitable arrangement for you?

Here is an example of a telephone conversation – Mrs Burns is trying to speak to her husband at his office. Pay special attention to the words in italics and then answer the questions that follow:

Receptionist: Central Insurance Office
Mrs Burns: Hello. Could I speak to Mr Burns, please – *extension* 23.
Receptionist: Is it a *business call* or a *private call*?
Mrs Burns: Well, actually it's a private call.
Receptionist: He's at an important conference and doesn't wish to be disturbed.
Mrs Burns: I know, but I'm his wife and it is rather *urgent*.
Receptionist: All right. *Hold on a moment* and *I'll put you through*. . . .
Hello Mrs Burns; I'm sorry, the number's *engaged*. Will you *hold the line* or do you want to *ring back*?

112

Mrs Burns:	No, I'll wait . . . .
Receptionist:	Hello. You can go ahead now.
Mr Carter:	Hello. Accounts Department.
Mrs Burns:	Hello. Is that Mr Carter?
Mr Carter:	*Speaking*. What can I do for you?
Mrs Burns:	Is Mr Burns *there* please?
Mr Carter:	No. *He's gone out* to an important meeting. If you want to see him you'll have to *make an appointment*.
Mrs Burns:	It's Mrs Burns here, and it's rather important. When *will he be back*?
Mr Carter:	Not for about an hour, I'm afraid. *Can I take a message?*
Mrs Burns:	Well, it's just that I've lost my keys and can't get into the house.
Mr Carter:	*I'm very sorry to hear that*. Don't worry, I'll try and get hold of him right away. Have you tried phoning the neighbours?
Mrs Burns:	No, *they're away* on holiday. I'm sorry to have troubled you like this.
Mr Carter:	*That's all right*. It could happen to anyone. I'll get the keys sent to you as quickly as possible. 'Bye for now.

EXERCISE 117

Give short answers:
1) What kind of call is Mrs Burns making?
2) Why is her call urgent?
3) Why does the receptionist ask her to hold the line?
4) Who answers the phone when the receptionist puts her through?
5) Where is Mr Burns?
6) What do you have to do if you want to see him?
7) Does Mr Carter expect him back soon?
8) What does Mr Carter offer to do?
9) Why can't Mrs Burns phone her neighbours?
10) What does Mr Carter promise to do in the end?

EXERCISE 118

Copy and complete these sentences:
1) 'Can I make ___ ___ to see Dr Evans tomorrow, please?'
   'Yes of course. Would 9.30 ___ you?'
   'No, after 10 o'clock would be more ___ .'
2) 'Can I ___ to Susie, please?'
   'I'm afraid she isn't ___ . Can I take ___ ___ or would you like to ___ ___ later?'
3) 'Can I have ___ 52 please?'
   '___ on a moment and I'll ___ ___ ___ .'
4) 'Hello operator. I must make an ___ call to my father but I haven't any money. I want to ___ ___ ___ .'

5) 'Thanks very much for explaining the mistake in my insurance form. I'm sorry ___ ___ ___ ___ .'
6) 'Hello, is that Home Computers?' 'No it isn't. I'm afraid ___ ___ ___ ___ ___ .'

EXERCISE 119

Using the phrases in the previous conversation, write down what you think Mike says in the following dialogue:

Mrs James: 9921 (double nine two one)
1) Mike: ___ ___ ___ ___ ___ ___ ___ ?
Mrs James: Speaking.
2) Mike: ___ ___ ___ ?
Mrs James: Cathy? No, I'm afraid she's gone out. Would you like to have a word with Emma instead?
3) Mike: ___ ___ ; ___ ___ ___ ___ .
Mrs James: No, it's no trouble. Hang on a moment and I'll go and call her.
4) Mike: ___ ___ ___ .
Emma: Hello, Mike. How are you?
5) Mike: ___ ___ , ___ ___ . ___ ___ ___ ?
Emma: Not very well actually. I've got a terrible headache.
6) Mike: ___ ___ ___ ___ ___ . ___ ___ ___ ___ ?
Emma: I don't expect she'll be back until midnight.
7) Mike: ___ ___ ___ ___ ___ ___ ?
Emma: No, you had better not do that; you might wake my parents.
8) Mike: ___ ___ ___ ___ ___ ___ , ___ ?
Emma: Yes, of course. Hang on a moment while I get a pencil.
9) Mike: ___ ___ ___ ___ ___ ___ ___ ___ ___ .
Emma: I see. You'd like her to ring you back at the office tomorrow.
10) Mike: ___ ___ ___ ___ ___ ___ ___ ___ ___ ___ ___ ___ ___ .
Emma: And you want to know what day would suit her for the tennis match.
11) Mike: ___ ___ . ___ ___ ___ ___ ___ ___ .
Emma: That's all right. Hope to see you soon. Goodbye for now.

Irregular verbs

Here is a list of the important irregular verbs. They are in alphabetical order so that you can find them quickly.

Present infinitive	Past	Past participle	Present infinitive	Past	Past participle
arise	arose	arisen	fling	flung	flung
awake	awoke	awoke/awakened	fly	flew	flown
be	was	been	forbid	forbade	forbidden
beat	beat	beaten	forget	forgot	forgotten
become	became	become	forgive	forgave	forgiven
begin	began	begun	freeze	froze	frozen
bend	bent	bent	get	got	got
bind	bound	bound	give	gave	given
bite	bit	bitten	go	went	gone
bleed	bled	bled	grind	ground	ground
blow	blew	blown	grow	grew	grown
break	broke	broken	hang	hung	hung
bring	brought	brought	have	had	had
build	built	built	hear	heard	heard
burn	burnt	burnt	hide	hid	hidden
burst	burst	burst	hit	hit	hit
buy	bought	bought	hold	held	held
catch	caught	caught	hurt	hurt	hurt
choose	chose	chosen	keep	kept	kept
cling	clung	clung	kneel	knelt	knelt
come	came	come	know	knew	known
cost	cost	cost	lay	laid	laid
creep	crept	crept	lead	led	led
cut	cut	cut	leap	leapt	leapt
deal	dealt	dealt	learn	learnt	learnt
dig	dug	dug	leave	left	left
do	did	done	lend	lent	lent
draw	drew	drawn	let	let	let
dream	dreamt	dreamt	lie	lay	lain
drink	drank	drunk	lie (fib)	lied	lied
drive	drove	driven	light	lit	lit
dwell	dwelt	dwelt	lose	lost	lost
eat	ate	eaten	make	made	made
fall	fell	fallen	mean	meant	meant
feed	fed	fed	meet	met	met
feel	felt	felt	mistake	mistook	mistaken
fight	fought	fought	pay	paid	paid
find	found	found	put	put	put
flee	fled	fled	read	read	read

Present infinitive	Past	Past participle	Present infinitive	Past	Past participle
ride	rode	ridden	split	split	split
ring	rang	rung	spoil	spoilt	spoilt
rise	rose	risen	spread	spread	spread
run	ran	run	spring	sprang	sprung
saw	sawed	sawn	stand	stood	stood
say	said	said	steal	stole	stolen
see	saw	seen	stick	stuck	stuck
seek	sought	sought	sting	stung	stung
sell	sold	sold	stink	stank	stunk
send	sent	sent	strike	struck	struck
set	set	set	swear	swore	sworn
sew	sewed	sewn	sweep	swept	swept
shake	shook	shaken	swell	swelled	swollen
shine	shone	shone	swim	swam	swum
shoot	shot	shot	swing	swung	swung
show	showed	shown	take	took	taken
shrink	shrank	shrunk	teach	taught	taught
shut	shut	shut	tear	tore	torn
sing	sang	sung	tell	told	told
sink	sank	sunk	think	thought	thought
sit	sat	sat	throw	threw	thrown
sleep	slept	slept	thrust	thrust	thrust
slide	slid	slid	tread	trod	trodden
smell	smelt	smelt	understand	understood	understood
speak	spoke	spoken	wake	woke	woken
speed	sped	sped	wear	wore	worn
spell	spelt	spelt	weep	wept	wept
spend	spent	spent	win	won	won
spill	spilt	spilt	wind	wound	wound
spin	spun	spun	wring	wrung	wrung
spit	spat	spat	write	wrote	written

Note

1) Some verbs ending –l, –m, –n can have –ed instead of –t in the past forms. Here are some examples: burn/dream/dwell/lean/learn/sew/show/smell/spell/spill/spoil.

2) The present infinitive of 'read' is pronounced like 'reed', but the past forms are pronounced like 'red'.

List of Teaching Words

ADJECTIVE: describing words added to nouns to tell you more about them, e.g. 'a girl (noun only) but a *pretty* girl (adjective + noun).

ADVERB: words which modify or add to the meaning of verbs or adjectives e.g. 'she walked' (verb) but she walked *quickly* (verb + adverb). Adverbs tell you *how* something is done, e.g. she read *slowly*, and they are often formed by adding *-ly* to the adjective, e.g. quick → quick*ly*, angry → angri*ly*.

ARTICLE: there are two sorts of article: definite (the) and indefinite (a/an). *The* denotes a special thing, e.g. '*the* book' means a particular book, but '*a* book' means *any* book.

AUXILIARY VERBS: also known as modal or helping verbs; they assist the main verb in the sentence, e.g. 'I *have* to go': *have* is the auxiliary to 'to go' and shows that the action is necessary.

CLAUSE: part of a sentence which contains a verb, e.g. in 'she liked the book which I gave to her', 'which I gave to her' forms the clause.

COMPARATIVE: used when describing or comparing two or more people or things, e.g. The boy is *shorter than* the girl.

CONJUNCTION: connecting words that join sentences or parts of sentences together, e.g. It was raining *and* snowing – *and* is the joining word.

CONSONANT: any letter of the alphabet except A E I O U (which are vowels).

DIRECT SPEECH: when one person says something directly to another, e.g. He said to Jane, 'Will you come out with me tonight?' The direct speech are the words contained in the inverted commas (see PUNCTUATION).

GERUND: this is formed by the verb + *ing* (often used in place of the infinitive) e.g to watch (infinitive) → watch*ing* (gerund), to like → lik*ing*.

INDIRECT SPEECH, see REPORTED SPEECH

INFINITIVE: this is found by placing 'to' before the present tense of the first person singular of any verb, e.g. to + laugh = to laugh (or to cry, to love etc).

MODAL VERBS, see AUXILIARY VERBS

NEGATIVE: the negative literally means the opposite of the positive, e.g. I am tall (positive) but I am *not* tall (negative). It implies denial, displeasure etc with things or persons, e.g. I am *not* pleased with your work means that it is *not good* work.

NOUN: words which are used to name a person or thing, e.g. book, girl, horse.

PAST PARTICIPLE: when you want to change the simple present into the simple past tense of a verb, you form it by using the past participle, e.g. dance→danced, fight→fought. How the past participle of a verb is formed depends on whether a verb is regular or irregular.

PHRASE: part of a sentence without a verb, e.g. They said goodbye at the station, 'at the station' is a phrase.

POSITIVE, see NEGATIVE.

PREPOSITION: words which show the relation between a noun or pronoun and another word in the sentence, e.g. He sat *on* the chair; she gave the record *to* me.

PRONOUN: literally words which stand in place of a noun, e.g. The girl is swimming→*she* is swimming. That is my hat → that is *mine*.

PUNCTUATION: any writing that you do is not complete without the correct punctuation. Here are the main signs: full stop = . comma = , colon = : semi-colon = ; question mark = ? exclamation mark = ! inverted commas = ' ' or " " apostrophe = ' hyphen = - brackets = ( ).

REFLEXIVE PRONOUNS: pronouns which refer to the subject of the sentence and are used to avoid repetition of that word, e.g. Sheila is looking at Sheila in the mirror → Sheila is looking at *herself* in the mirror. *Herself* is the reflexive pronoun.

RELATIVE PRONOUNS: words which describe nouns which come immediately before them. They are used to distinguish that noun from any others that might occur in the sentence, e.g. The boy *who* laughed at you was my brother, 'who' is the relative pronoun.

REPORTED SPEECH: used when the meaning of the words stays the same but the words are being spoken by another person, e.g. He boasted, 'I can speak Russian', but *you* would report his words by saying: He boasted that he could speak Russian.

SENTENCE: all the words between two full stops. A sentence must have a noun/pronoun and a verb and it usually contains many other parts of speech (e.g. adjectives, conjunctions etc).

SUPERLATIVE: used when describing or comparing three or more people or things, e.g. She is *the tallest* girl that I have seen; he is *the worst* behaved boy in the class.

TENSE: different forms of a verb, e.g. they are here (present tense), they were not listening (past continuous tense).

VERB: words telling or stating what the subject is *doing*, e.g. walk, play.

VOWEL: the letters A E I O U are vowels. Every word is made up of both vowels and consonants (see also CONSONANTS).

Answers

Exercise 1
1) Mr Burns. 2) In the bathroom. 3) . . . making . . .
4) . . . making coffee? 5) . . . reading the . . . 6) . . .
reading the paper? 7) . . . he . . . 8) . . . he is. 9) . . .
he isn't. 10) Yes she is. 11) No she isn't. 12) Yes . . .
13) No it isn't. 14) No it isn't. 15) Yes it is. 16) No it
isn't. 17) . . . is . . . 18) . . . is . . . A paper. 19) . . . is
Grandpa . . . 20) . . . is Mrs Burns . . . 21) . . . is the
cat drinking? 22) . . . is Mrs Burns . . .

Exercise 2
Derek: . . . I'm putting on my shoes.
Sandra: . . . I'm getting up.
Grandpa: . . . I'm reading the . . .
Grandpa: . . . I am.
Grandpa: . . . I'm smoking a . . .
Mrs Burns: I'm making some . . .

Exercise 3
1) I'm studying English. 2) I'm sitting down. 3) I'm
sitting in the . . . 4) I'm sitting on a chair. 5) I'm using
a . . . 6) Yes, I am. *or* No, I'm not. 7) I'm wearing a
. . . 8) Yes, it is. *or* No, it isn't.

Exercise 4
1) He sells bread. 2) He plays the piano. 3) He plays
football. 4) He delivers the letters. 5) He delivers
milk. 6) They sell cigarettes, tobacco. 7) They fly
planes. 8) They clean windows. 9) They drive
ambulances.

Exercise 5
1) He always smokes a pipe after dinner. 2) She hardly
ever goes to the cinema. 3) They always wear uniforms. 4) He usually watches television. 5) She
seldom wears her crown. 6) We occasionally go to a
restaurant.
Note that in (2) and (5) you may use 'hardly ever',
'seldom' or 'rarely' without altering the meaning of the
sentence. In (6) you could use 'sometimes', as the degree of
frequency is very close to 'occasionally'.

Exercise 6
1) Mrs Burns is a housewife. She always does the
washing-up at about 8.30 and tidies up the house. She
usually makes the beds at 9 o'clock. At 10 o'clock she
generally goes shopping and at 11 o'clock she often visits
a friend. She has a snack lunch at 1 o'clock and usually
gets home before 4 o'clock.
2) Derek is a mechanic. He always gets on his bike at
about 8.30 and rides off to work. He usually arrives at the
garage at 9 o'clock. At 10 o'clock he generally repairs
cars and at 11 o'clock he often has a tea-break. He has

some sandwiches for lunch at 1 o'clock and sometim[es]
gets home at 6 o'clock.
3) Sandra is a pupil at school. She always goes ou[t]
about 8.30 and catches a bus. She usually starts
classes at 9 o'clock. At 10 o'clock she generally ha[s a]
music lesson and at 11 o'clock she often buys so[me]
sweets. She has lunch in the school canteen at 1 o'cl[ock]
and always gets home at a quarter past four.
4) Grandpa is retired. He always goes outside at 8[.30]
and does some gardening. He usually has a cigarette [at 10]
o'clock. At 10 o'clock he generally goes for a walk an[d at]
11 o'clock he often meets a friend. He has lunch in a [pub]
at 1 o'clock and rarely gets back home before half p[ast]
five.

Exercise 7
List A: Sugar, beer, rice, tobacco, cheese, pe[as,]
spaghetti, tea.
List B: Cars, sausages, cups of tea, cigarettes, bottle[s of]
wine, children, people.

Exercise 8
There is some salt and there is some sugar, some rice [and]
some onions. There are four tins of soup and a packe[t of]
spaghetti.

Exercise 9
1) There isn't much beer. There is only a li[ttle.]
2) There aren't many tomatoes. There are only a f[ew.]
3) There isn't much bread. There's only a li[ttle.]
4) There aren't many sausages. There are only a [few.]
5) There are three. 6) How much cheese is there in [the]
fridge? 7) How much milk is there in the fri[dge?]
8) How many bottles of beer are there in the fri[dge?]
9) How much fish is there in the fridge? 10) How m[any]
tomatoes are there in the fridge?

Exercise 10
They need some eggs, some milk, some beer and s[ome]
fish.
They don't need any cheese, any tobacco or any chic[ken.]

Exercise 11
1) Yes there is. 2) No there isn't. 3) No there i[sn't.]
4) Yes there is. 5) Yes there are. 6) No there ar[en't.]
7) No there aren't. 8) Yes there are. 9) No t[here]
aren't.

Exercise 12
1) It is an old lady's hat. 2) It's a policeman's hel[met.]
These helmets belong to policemen. They['re]
policemen's helmets. 3) This hat belongs to a clow[n.]

clown's hat. These hats belong to clowns. They are
vns' hats. 4) Those helmets belong to astronauts.
ey are astronauts' helmets. 5) That crown belongs
he Queen. It's the Queen's crown. 6) Those hats
ong to sailors. They are sailors' hats. 7) It's the
boy's. 8) It's the old lady's. 9) They are the
cemen's. 10) Whose hats are those? 11) The
vn's.

rcise 13
t's hers. It belongs to her. 2) It's ours. It belongs to
3) It's yours. It belongs to you. 4) They are
ey're) his. They belong to him. 5) They're mine.
y belong to me. 6) It's theirs. It belongs to them.

rcise 14 (Police sergeant's replies)
. man called Stubbs. 2) Joe. 3) He's sixty. 4) He
short hair and he is ugly. 5) Yes he is. 6) He hasn't
a job. He's a thief. 7) He's a bank robber. 8) In
chester. 9) He lives in Dublin. 10) It's about 300
s. 11) Yes it is. 12) 10th September 1977.

rcise 15
: is Tuesday. 2) It's ten to ten in one picture, and
ity past ten in the other. 3) She is 17. 4) She lives
Bath Road. 5) No she doesn't. 6) No she doesn't.
o they aren't. 8) Yes she can. 9) Yes she can.

rcise 16
. . than Fiona. 2) . . . than Fiona. 3) . . . than
idy. 4) Fiona . . . than Mandy. 5) Fiona is . . .
Mandy. 6) Mandy . . . Fiona. 7) Fiona . . . than
idy. 8) . . . than Mandy. 9) Mandy . . . Fiona.
. . than Fiona. 11) . . . speak French and Italian
12) . . . speak French or Italian . . . 13) . . .
er the phone . . . 14) . . . use a photocopier . . .
Fiona.

rcise 17
. she is . . . 2) . . . she can speak more . . . 3) . . .
vants to do more . . . 4) . . . she can't take notes
.

rcise 18
andy has more cats than Fiona. 2) Mandy has
: coats than Fiona. 3) Mandy weighs less than
a (Mandy is less heavy than Fiona). 4) Mandy has
er hair than Fiona. 5) Mandy has fewer sisters
Fiona. 6) Mandy is shorter than Fiona.
andy has more money in the bank than Fiona.
andy has more records than Fiona.

cise 19
ne old lady is going to get into the car. 3) The
r is going to start the engine. 4) He's going to turn
ner. 5) He's going to drive over a bridge. 6) He's
; to go through a tunnel. 7) Some people are going
lk across the road. 8) The car is going to slow
i behind a lorry. 9) It's going to overtake the lorry
rash into a bus. 10) The cases are going to fall off
oof.

cise 20
ne boat is going to go under the bridge. 2) The

driver is going to slow down. 3) The bus-driver is
going to shout at the taxi-driver. 4) She is going to get
out of the taxi.

Exercise 21
1) . . . the drawer. 2) It is in the . . . 3) . . . on the
table. 4) . . . the wall. 5) . . . in front of Bert. 6) . . .
standing behind the door. 7) . . . outside the room.
8) . . . going to . . . 9) . . . going to . . . 10) . . . going
to . . . 11) . . . going to . . . 12) . . . going to take him
to . . . 13) No he doesn't. 14) . . . going to steal things.

Exercise 22
1) The jewels are *in* the drawer. 2) Bert is going to *put*
his gloves *on*. 3) The lady is standing *behind* the door.
4) The clock is going to strike in *two* minutes. 5) Bert is
going to *steal* a fur coat. 6) Bert is going to *take* a picture
off the wall. 7) *The policeman* is going to arrest *Bert*.
8) The lady is going to hit him with *a vase of flowers*.
9) Bert is going to *take* the jewels *out of* the drawer.
10) Bert is going to spend two years *in prison*.

Exercise 23
1) A tall, dark man. 2) Yes she is. 3) No she isn't.
4) She is going to have a lot of accidents. 5) . . .
accidents. 6) . . . after a long time. 7) . . . give the
fortune-teller any money. 8) . . . another girl. 9) . . .
have a lot of bad luck. 10) . . . angry.

Exercise 24
1) . . . film. 2) . . . David. 3) . . . magazine. 4) . . .
fish. 5) . . . record.

Exercise 25
1) a She stayed at home. b She went to the cinema. c She
went to the hairdresser's. 2) a She spent £60. b £1.00.
c £8.50. 3) a She ate some fish. b She drank some wine.
4) a No she didn't. b No she didn't. c Yes she did.

Exercise 26
1) What did you do on Friday? 2) How much did you
spend in the restaurant? 3) Who did you meet at the
disco? 4) What did you read at the hairdresser's?
5) How much did the hat cost? 6) What did you do
yesterday? 7) When did you meet David? 8) Where
did you go on Tuesday?

Exercise 27
1) a Maria. b Hans. c Maria. d Hans. e Greta. f Hans.
2) By boat. 3) Hans travelled on the underground,
Maria travelled by car. 4) She thought it was the most
beautiful park in the world, and the cheapest. 5) At
Hampton Court. 6) It was the worst hotel in London.
7) She thought it was the finest cathedral in Europe.
8) Double Gloucester cheese. 9) Mt. Snowdon.
10) Maria was the luckiest; Hans the unluckiest.
11) She bought some cheap clothes and souvenirs.
12) With an English family. 13) At Hampton Court.
14) The castles and the scenery. 15) She took a lot of
photos. 16) . . . it was both beautiful and cheap.
17) . . . he couldn't understand his English. 18) . . .
the banks closed at 3.30. 19) . . . the pubs closed at
10.30 and the buses stopped running at about eleven
o'clock. 20) . . . he had a terrible time.

Exercise 28

Three men *went* to have lunch in a cafe *at* one o'clock *on* Saturday. They *weren't* very hungry and *didn't have* much to eat. Tom and Jerry *had* sandwiches. Fred *wanted* to have fish and chips but there *wasn't* any and the waiter *gave* him a meat pie instead. After lunch they *drank* some coffee and *smoked* cigarettes *for* a few minutes. *At* about five past two the waiter *brought* them the bill. It *was* exactly £3.00. '*Did you enjoy* your meal?' he *asked*. 'Yes I *did*', *replied* Fred, 'but it *was* an expensive pie.' Each man *gave* the waiter £1.00 and then *put* on their coats.
A moment later the waiter *came* back and *said*: 'I'm very sorry, I *made* a mistake just now; your bill *came* to only £2.50 and not £3.00.' So he *put* 50p back on the table. The men *thought* for a few moments because they *couldn't* divide 50p between three people. Eventually they *took* 10p each and *left* the waiter 20p as a tip because he *was* very honest.
They *went* out of the cafe, and then Fred suddenly *looked* worried. 'How much *did you pay*, Tom?'
'First I *paid* £1.00, then the waiter *gave* me back 10p. So the meal *cost* me 90p.'
'Well, Jerry *paid* 90p and I did too. That makes £2.70.'
'That's right.'
'How much *did we leave* for the waiter?'
'20p.'
'That makes £2.90. I *thought* we *gave* the waiter £3.00. Where's the other 10p?'

Exercise 29

2) . . . he drives a car. 3) . . . now he has a moustache. 4) . . . but now he wears a suit. 5) . . . but now he is rich. 6) He used to be single . . . 7) . . . but now he is . . . 8) He used to be thin . . . 9) . . . now he smokes cigars. 10) He used to read . . .

Exercise 30

1) *b* He has (he's) won the race. *c* He has scored a goal. *d* He has bought a sports car. *e* He has found a £5 note. 2) *g* She has (she's) cut her finger. *h* She has broken a vase. *i* She has fallen over. *j* She has dropped an icecream.

Exercise 31

2) They have swept the carpets. 3) They have emptied the ashtrays. 4) They have folded up the newspapers. 5) They have polished the silver. 6) They have dusted the shelves. 7) They have closed the windows. 8) They have put away the books.

Exercise 32

1) How many cups of coffee have you drunk this week? 2) . . . films have you seen . . . 3) . . . books have you read . . . 4) . . . cakes have you eaten. . . . 5) . . . letters have you written . . . 6) . . . phone calls have you made . . . 7) . . . sugar have you used . . . 8) . . . money have you spent . . . 9) . . . petrol have you used . . . 10) . . . coca-cola have you drunk . . .

Exercise 33

1) Sandra wants to *read the newspaper; she hasn't read it yet.*

2) Derek doesn't want to see the Tower of London; *he* seen it already.
Sandra wants to *see the Tower of London; she hasn* seen it yet.
3) Derek doesn't need any skiing lessons; he's had *som* already.
Sandra needs *skiing lessons; she hasn't had any yet*
4) Derek doesn't want any coffee; *he's had some alread*
Sandra wants *some coffee; she hasn't had any yet.*

Exercise 34

1) They have been living in their house for six year They have been living there since 19—. 2) I have bee learning English for two months. I have been learning since . . . 3) He has been driving his car for ni months. He has been driving it since . . . 4) She h been waiting at the bus stop for forty minutes. She been waiting there since 10.15. 5) He has been eati lunch for forty-five minutes. He's been eating since o'clock. 6) He's been reading a novel for five days. H has been reading it since Monday.

Exercise 35

1) It has been running. 2) He has been swimmir 3) He has been cutting the grass. 4) It has been eatin fish. 5) He has been fighting. 6) He has been waiti for a long time.

Exercise 36

1) *a* love, enjoy. *b* trips. *c* abroad. *d* lose their tempe *e* chat. *f* ugly. *g* horrible. *h* polite. 2) Ninety years o 3) Because the producer has invited her for an int view. 4) Two. 5) In London. 6) The buildin snack-bars and supermarkets. 7) She thinks people a friendlier than they used to be. 8) They used to sh and boo. 9) More than fifty years ago. 10 *a* A singer dancer. *b* When people threw tomatoes at the acto *c* She wants to go to Hollywood.

Exercise 37

1) She was speaking on the phone. 2) No, she did 3) No, she wasn't. 4) He was putting up a pict (using a hammer). 5) He was holding a hamm 6) Yes, he was. 7) He was watching television (T 8) They were listening to a record. 9) It was raini 10) He was carrying an umbrella. 11) No. 12 motor-bike. 13) Because they were all making a lo noise.

Exercise 38

1) himself. 2) themselves. 3) myself. 4) ourselv 5) each other. 6) each other. 7) himself. 8) e other.

Exercise 39

1) After they had shaken hands, they sat down. 2) soon as the cowboy had entered the bar, he immedia shot the barman. 3) When Fred had eaten s shepherd's pie, he had some rice pudding. 4) As s as he had drunk a glass of brandy, he choked. 5) A the thief had robbed a bank, broken into a house stolen a car, the police arrested him. 6) Dick's b sacked him because he hadn't done any work. 7)

dn't ask Sue to dance with him because he'd forgotten
er name. 8) When Mike had filled his car with petrol,
e drove off. 9) As soon as the waiter had opened a
ottle of champagne, he poured out a drink. 10) After
e had switched off the light, he went to bed.

xercise 40

1 He told me he wanted some beer. 2) He told me he
dn't understand that problem. 3) He told me he had
roken those plates the day before. 4) He told me I
adn't phoned the week before. 5) He told me they had
on the match. 6) He told me he hadn't had any
reakfast. 7) He told me I was going to be late. 8) He
old me Sam was going to buy a car on that day. 9) He
old me he had been going to cross the road when he had
en a sports car coming. 10) He told me he had been
udying English for four months. 11) He told me I
ouldn't drive. 12) He told me Tom would be late if he
dn't hurry. 13) He told me he wouldn't forget to post
y letter. 14) He told me he had to wait there for
ally. 15) He told me I should change my job.
.B. *The word 'that' may be put after the phrase 'He told
e' in all these sentences, and ought to be so placed when
ey are written down, not spoken.*

xercise 41

. where to stand. . . . where to hit the ball. . . . what
do. . . . what to wear. . . . when to stand near the
et. . . . when to hit the ball. . . . who to play with. . . .
ow to score. . . . how to hold the racquet. . . . whether
stand near the net. . . . how many balls to play with.
Ie might not even know how to hit the ball!)

xercise 42

1 b. 2) a. 3) c. 4) c. 5) b. 6) c. 7) c. 8) *Sandra*:
b, e, f, h. *mother*: c, d, g. 9) Three weeks. 10) If she
ays in a 5-star hotel.

xercise 43

Because it is too high for him to reach. Because he is
ot tall enough. 3) Because it is too expensive for him
buy. Because he isn't rich enough. 4) Because it's too
nall for him to wear. Because he isn't small enough.
Because it's too narrow for her to get through.
ecause she isn't slim enough. 6) Because it is too cold
r him to swim. Because it isn't warm enough.

xercise 44

. . . catch a fish. 2) . . . break. 3) . . . fall into the
ver. 4) . . . he will probably . . . 5) It may sting the
an. 6) . . . wake up. 7) . . . may/might. . . 8) She is
out to light it. 9) She is about to eat it. 10) . . . to
in. 11) . . . will probably . . . might . . . unlikely
. . .

xercise 45

Everybody . . . 2) Nobody . . . 3) Somebody . . .
Nobody. . . 5) . . . anyone . . . someone . . . 6) . . .
aybody . . . everybody . . . 7) . . . anything . . .
mething . . . 8) . . . anything . . . something . . .
. . . something . . . nothing. 10 . . . anybody . . .
eryone . . .

Exercise 46

1) . . . will be . . . 2) . . . was going to . . .) . . . was
going to . . . 4) . . . shan't/won't be . . .; I'll be . . .
5) . . . will be . . . 6) . . . was going to . . . 7) . . . will
be . . . 8) . . . was going to . . .

Exercise 47

thinking; to stop; to do; trying; crying; lying; getting;
feel; reading; looking; taking; to spend; reading; taking;
to have; reading; sleeping; to make; feel; going; getting;
improve; reading; looking; to join; to show; joining;
take; helping; choose; going; find.

Exercise 48

1) Maria *is fond of* reading ghost stories. 2) Detective
stories are *easy* to read. 3) *Joining a library is free.*
4) Sally want to take Maria some *detective* stories.
5) Jane says Maria *dislikes* reading magazines. 6) Sally
thinks ghost stories will *prevent Maria from sleeping.*

Exercise 49

1) She likes ghost stories. 2) She dislikes magazines.
3) Because she can't help crying. 4) Because she was
going down a steep slope. 5a) Jane. 5b) Sally.
5c) Maria.

Exercise 50

1) He has to clean his rifle. 2) He has to polish his
boots. 3) He has to wear a uniform. 4) He has to get up
at 6 am. 5) He has to peel the potatoes. 6) He has to
salute the officers.

Exercise 51

1) He must load his rifle. 2) He must fire at the enemy.
3) He must put on a helmet. 4) He has got to make him
a bandage. 5) He has got to give him some water.
6) He has got to get him to hospital.

Exercise 52

1) He needn't clean his shoes. 2) He needn't wear a
uniform 3) He needn't cook breakfast. 4) He needn't
carry a rifle.

Exercise 53

1) He ought to give it to the man. 2) He ought to offer
her his seat. 3) He ought to give a sweet to the child.
4) He ought to go to bed.

Exercise 54

1) He had better warn the neighbours. 2) He had better
close the windows. 3) He had better lock all the doors.
4) He had better call the police. 5) He had better give it
something to eat.

Exercise 55

1) They had better not play the record-player. 2) They
had better not turn on the TV (television). 3) They had
better not talk too loudly. 4) They had better not slam
the door. 5) They had better not open the window.

Exercise 56

1) You should go to the hairdresser. 2) You should put
on some make-up. 3) You should stop smoking.
4) You should buy some elegant shoes. 5) You should
look more cheerful. 6) You should wear contact lenses.

122

Exercise 57

1) You mustn't stroke the lion. 2) You mustn't feed the monkeys. 3) You mustn't touch the snake. 4) You mustn't throw your ball at the seal. 5) You mustn't pull the tiger's tail.

Exercise 58

1) You shouldn't wear a suit in the kitchen. 2) You shouldn't drop eggs on the floor. 3) You shouldn't put plates on the cooker. 4) You shouldn't put salt in the milk.

Exercise 59

1) You shouldn't have broken the plates; you should have put them on the table. 2) You shouldn't have burnt the toast; you should have watched it. 3) You shouldn't have let the milk boil over; you should have watched it. 4) You shouldn't have let the sink overflow; you should have turned off the tap.

Exercise 60

1) He must be rich. 2) He must be poor. 3) He must be about fifty. He can't be less than forty-five. 4) He must be about twenty. He can't be more than twenty-five. 5) He must have a chauffeur. 6) He must have read a lot of books. 7) He must be hungry. 8) He must eat a lot. 9) He must live in a mansion. 10) He must be short-sighted.

Exercise 61

1) a) Tyres are made of rubber. b) Sweaters are made of wool. c) Mirrors are made of glass. d) Shoes are made of leather. 2) a) Bread is made from flour. b) Wine is made from grapes. c) Omelettes are made from eggs. d) Porridge is made from oats. 3) a) A car is usually kept in a garage. b) Dresses are usually kept in a wardrobe. c) Pound notes are usually kept in a wallet. d) Matches are usually kept in a matchbox. 4) a) Soap is used for washing. b) A kettle is used for boiling water. c) Bricks are used for building. d) Toothpaste is used for cleaning teeth. 5) a) Napoleon was born in Corsica. b) Shakespeare was born in England. c) President Roosevelt was born in America. 6) a) Brazil was discovered by Pedro Cabral. b) America was discovered by Columbus. c) New Zealand was discovered by Captain Cooke. 7) a) The railway engine was invented by Stephenson. b) Penicillin was invented by Fleming. c) Television was invented by Baird. 8) a) Archduke Ferdinand of Austria was assassinated in 1914. b) Ghandi was assassinated in 1948. c) John F. Kennedy was assassinated in 1963. 9) a) Kimonos are worn in Japan. b) Kilts are worn in Scotland. c) Ponchos are worn in Mexico. d) Saris are worn in India. 10) a) Paella is eaten in Spain. b) Stroganov is eaten in Russia. c) Ghoulash is eaten in Hungary. d) Frogs' legs are eaten in France.

Exercise 62

1) He is usually fed four times a day. 2) He has just been taken into the bathroom. 3) He is being given a bath. 4) His hair ought to be washed. 5) He is going t be dried in a moment. 6) His hair must be cut soor 7) He will (He'll) be taken out in his pram if it stop raining 8) He must be kept warm. 9) He will (He'll be put to bed at 7 o'clock. 10) She is never allowed t rest.

Exercise 63

1) I'm going to have my house painted. 2) I'm going t have my windows cleaned. 3) I'm going to have m shoes mended. 4) I'm going to have my grass cu 5) I'm going to have my nails manicured. 6) I'm goin to have my baggage sent to my hotel. 7) I'm going have my suit dry cleaned. 8) I'm going to have my eye tested.

Exercise 64

1) a A butcher is someone who sells meat. b A chemist someone who sells medicine. c A newsagent is someor who sells newspapers and magazines. d A greengrocer someone who sells fruit and vegetables. e A bu conductor is someone who sells bus tickets.
2) a A nurse is someone who looks after patients in hospital. b A baby-sitter is someone who looks aft children in a house (when the parents are out for th evening). c A caretaker is someone who looks after building. d A courier is someone who looks after touris in a bus. e A cloakroom attendant is someone who loo after coats in a theatre or restaurant.
3) a A cow is an animal which gives us milk. b A hen is bird that gives us eggs. c A silkworm is an animal which gives us silk. d A mink is an animal which gives expensive fur. e A pig is an animal which gives us me (bacon).
Note that 'which' could be replaced by 'that' when the sentences are used in speech.
4) a Brazil is a country which is famous for coffe b Saudi Arabia is a country which is famous for o c Ghana is a country which is famous for cocoa. d Irelar is a country which is famous for potatoes. e Jamaica is country which is famous for bananas.

Exercise 65

1) Jack is the boy she spoke to. 2) Jack is the boy she fond of. 3) Jack is the boy she shouted at. 4) Jack is t boy she feels sorry for. 5) Jack is the boy she argu with. 6) Jack is the boy she played tennis with. 7) Ja is the boy she talked about. 8) Jack is the boy she tired of.

Exercise 66

1) . . . town which is situated . . . 2) . . . George I who built . . . 3) . . . beach, which is covered . 4) . . . shellfish, which you can buy under . . . 5) . piers, one of which has been . . . 6) . . . place behi the Palace Pier which is famous for antiques. 7) . Railway, which are alongside the beach, are . . 8) . . . Brighton, many of whom are students who university . . . 9) . . . people, some of whom are . 10) Graham Greene, who is a writer, thinks Brighton the strangest place he has been to.

Exercise 67

) I hurt my knee while playing football. 2) She felt ervous while she was having a driving lesson. 3) He ʼas ill while he was on holiday. 4) He fell asleep while ʼe was having a history lesson. 5) Let's tidy the office ʼuring his absence. 6) During the party he got drunk.) He felt sick during the play.

Exercise 68

) He's deaf, so he can't hear you. 2) He's short-ghted, so he can't see you. 3) He's short, so he can't ʼach the top shelf. 4) He's very fat, so he can't run ʼst. 5) As I've overslept, I'll be late. 6) As he's very ʼean, he won't buy you a present. 7) As she's very ʼnd, I'm sure she'll help you. 8) As the children are ʼry clever, I expect they'll pass their exams.

Exercise 69

) . . . since/because there has (there's) been a rail strike.) . . . since/because there has been a flu epidemic.) . . . because the pitch is wet. 4) . . . since there has ʼen a dispute with the manager.

Exercise 70

ʼ . . . although he is rude. 2) . . . although he is bad-ʼmpered. 3) . . . although he is stupid. 4) . . . al-ʼough he is untidy. 5) . . . although he is mean.) . . . although he is unpopular. 7) . . in spite of the ʼin. 8) . . . despite having a cold. 9) . . . in spite of ʼaving a broken arm. 10) . . . in spite of the doctor's ʼder. 11) . . . in spite of the awful weather.

Exercise 71

ʼ . . . you want to light a fire. 3) . . . you feel cold. ʼ . . . you hurt yourself. 5) . . . you feel hungry. ʼ . . . you want to know the time.

Exercise 72

ʼ c. 2) h. 3) g. 4) a. 5) f. 6) e. 7) b. 8) d. 9) . . . ʼow the time. 10) . . . in order to keep dry. 11) . . . in ʼder to keep her hands warm. 12) . . . in order to see ʼtter (more clearly). 13) . . . in order to look more ʼtractive.
. . so as to . . . *may be used in all cases*.)

Exercise 73

ʼ I'm so tired that I can't keep my eyes open. 2) This ʼit is so expensive that he cannot afford it. 3) There's ʼch a lot of noise here that I can't hear you. 4) There ʼe so many people here that I can't move. 5) The ʼffee was so awful that I couldn't drink it. 6) She has ʼten such a lot of icecream that she feels sick. 7) I'm so ʼngry that I could eat a horse. 8) He has drunk such a ʼrge amount of (so much) beer that he can't walk ʼroperly. 9) . . . so many . . . such a . . . 10) . . . so ʼuch . . . 11) . . . so . . . such . . . 12) . . . so . . .

Exercise 74

ʼ You can use my phone provided that you don't . . .
ʼ You can borrow my umbrella so long as you give . . .
ʼ You can ride my horse so long as you don't . .
ʼ You can go for a swim provided that you don't . . .
ʼ You can have an ice-cream as long as you eat . . .

6) You can sit behind me . . . so long as you hold on tight.

Exercise 75

If you have more than three *a* answers you are a coward; more than three *b* answers means you are nervous or hysterical; more than three *c* answers indicates you are aggressive; more than three *d* answers means you are self-centred or a dreamer, and more than three *e* answers means you are scientific and have no feelings.

Exercise 76

1) If the pupils worked harder, they would (they'd) pass . . . 2) If I were the Prime Minister, I would cut . . . 3) If you drove more slowly, you wouldn't have . . . 4) If I lived on a desert island, I'd build . . . 5) If you were an astronaut, you would be . . . 6) I would be an interpreter, if I knew . . . 7) He would drive a taxi, if he had . . . 8) He wouldn't annoy his friends, if he didn't phone . . . 9) I would go to university if I were you. 10) I would go mad if I had a job . . .

Exercise 77

1) *a* knew; *b* had; *c* were. 2) *a* would; *b* would; *c* would. 3) *a* had; *b* hadn't; *c* had.

Exercise 78

2) If I had been . . . I would have cut . . . 3) If you had driven . . . you wouldn't have had . . . 4) If I had lived . . . I would have built . . . 5) If you had been . . . you would have been . . . 6) I would have been . . . if I had known . . . 7) He would have driven . . . if he had had . . . 8) He wouldn't have annoyed . . . if he hadn't phoned . . . 9) I would have gone . . . if I had been you. 10) I would have gone mad if I had had . . .

Exercise 79

1) . . . colour as her mother's. 2) . . . slim as her mother. 3) . . . weight as her mother. 4) . . . as her mother 5) . . . has the same colour eyes as his father. 6) . . . as her brother. 7) No, he has similar hair to his sister. 8) No, he is similar in size to his father. 9) No, his weight is similar to his father's. 10) . . . has Mrs Burns. 11) . . . is his father. 12) . . . does her daughter. 13) . . . does her brother. 14) . . . does his wife. 15) . . . nor has her mother. 16) . . . so is his sister.

Exercise 80

1) Both Mr Burns and Derek . . . 2) Both Sandra and Derek . . . 3) . . . has brown eyes. 4) All of the Burns family . . . 5) None of the Burns family . . .

Exercise 81

1) smells. 2) tastes. 3) feels. 4) talks like. 5) look like. 6) drives . . . like. 7) sounds like.

Exercise 82

1) or else. 2) however, 3) First of all . . . then . . . after that . . . to end with. 4) either . . . or . . . but . . 5) whether . . . or. 6) otherwise. 7) or else. 8) neither . . . nor . . . Nevertheless,

Exercise 83

1) Mary likes pop music. She can't stand the music of

Mozart. 2) An honest person tells the truth. The/A boy in the classroom told a lie. 3) Johnny has gone to school. At 4 pm his mother is going to the school to collect him. 4) This fork is dirty; can I have another one? 5) Some of the children are working, others are in the playground. 6) Is Jim playing football on the football pitch? No, he's playing the violin in the lounge. 7) He went for a swim and found a beautiful stone at the bottom of the sea. But when he took the stone out of the water, it lost its colour and he threw the stone back.

Exercise 84
(an asterisk * shows where *no* article is required)

St Ives is *a* beautiful old fishing-port on *the* North coast of Cornwall. It is built on *a* slope round *a* picturesque bay. *The* houses are jumbled together and *the* streets are narrow. *The* cars have to be parked in *carparks at *the* top of *a* hill.
The town is rich in*history. There is *a* legend that*St Ia came to*Cornwall from*Ireland in *the* fifth century in *a* tiny boat (*the* Irish say on *a* leaf!). He built *a* fortress on *an* island (which in true Irish fashion is no longer *an* island but joined to *the* mainland by*sand), and *the* town took his name. By *the* Middle Ages *the* name St Ia had changed to St Ives. It was developed as *a* fishing-port and became famous for*pilchards. *A* look-out man used to call out *the* fishermen when he saw *a* shoal of*fish. But by *the* end of *the* last century *the* fish had moved to *other waters.
At *the* same time, with *the* opening of *a* railway in *the* 1880s,*artists started moving into *the* fishermen's cottages. One of *the* most famous was Whistler and *another was Sickert. They found that *the* light suited them because it had high ultraviolet content. *The* town is still popular with*artists and has *a* great many attractions including *the* famous Leach Pottery and *the* only Museum of Cinematography in*Britain. To *the* east of *the* town there is *the* wonderful Birds' Paradise and *the* Children's Zoo. *The* Model Village nearby has *a* lot of attractions including *the* Museum of Smuggling. Unfortunately, *the* town is crowded with *tourists in *July and*August but it is still worth *a* visit. *The* inhabitants are particularly proud to have given *a* home to Barbara Hepworth, one of *the* most famous artists of *the* century, and now regard their town as *the* San Francisco of*England.

Exercise 85
1) do the polishing. 2) make an apple pie. 3) make a shopping list. 4) do some sewing. 5) do the ironing. 6) make an omelette. 7) do the washing-up. 8) make a sweater. 9) make home-made jam. 10) do some spring-cleaning.

Exercise 86
1) go red . . . get embarrassed. 2) tremble . . . get frightened. 3) cry . . . get upset. 4) scream . . . get angry. 5) go pale . . . get sick. 6) go wild . . . get excited.

Exercise 87
1) do up *or* button up. 2) fold up. 3) used up 4) unwrap . . . untie *or* undo. 5) roll up. 6) Eat up 7) washes up . . . dries up. 8) saving up. 9) tidy up

Exercise 88
1) switch on. 2) stick on. 3) pin on. 4) pin on *or* clip on. 5) nail on. 6) sew on.

Exercise 89
1) knocked off. 2) pushed off. 3) took off. 4) jumped off *or* got off. 5) fell off. 6) Keep off.

Exercise 90
1) drove off. 2) dashed off *or* rushed off. 3) chased off 4) send him off. 5) hurried off. 6) took off.

Exercise 91
1) I must sew it on. 2) I must wipe it off. 3) I must lock it up. 4) I must save (it) up. 5) I must cut it up (for him). 6) I must wrap it up, tie it up, stick it (the label) on. 7) I must write it down. 8) I must fold it up

Exercise 92
1) They cut down trees. 2) they knock down houses 3) They take off. 4) It drives on. 5) She takes down notes.

Exercise 93
1) The dog has eaten it up. 2) The dog has drunk it up. 3) The dog has knocked it off the table. 4) The dog has torn (chewed) it up. 5) John must clear it up

Exercise 94
1) tough. 2) rough. 3) harmful. 4) tough. 5) wonderful. 6) boring. 7) awful. 8) soft. 9) huge . . tiny. 10) mean.

Exercise 95
1) *a* lively; *b* noisy; *c* proud; *d* ridiculous; *e* old fashioned. 2) The English are eccentric and reserved the Scots are adventurous and cautious; the Welsh are musical, excitable and suspicious; the Irish are dreamy talkative and charming. 3) The Scots are thrifty, an they are inventive. 4) The English are reserved and th Irish are talkative.

Exercise 96
rainy; cloudy; windy; stormy; foggy; misty; sunny chilly; frosty; icy.

Exercise 97
1) Jane is fair-haired, blue-eyed and well-dressed 2) Fred is short-haired and bad-tempered. 3) Fred father is kind-hearted but old-fashioned. 4) H trousers were creased and his shoes were unpolished 5) The toast was burnt and the coffee unsweetened 6) The athlete is strong-willed but big-headed.

Exercise 98
1) self-centred. 2) self-conscious. 3) self-satisfied 4) self-critical. 5) self-made. 6) self-confiden 7) self-winding. 8) self-service.

xercise 99
) understaffed. 2) overworked. 3) underpaid.) underfed. 5) over-crowded. 6) They were under-)oked. 7) It was overdone. 8) under-ripe. 9 over-1arged. 10) overheated. 11) It had been overrated.

xercise 100
) exciting *or* thrilling. 2) amusing. 3) terrifying.) horrifying *or* shocking. 5) puzzling. 6) boring.) moving. 8) frightening. 9) annoying. 10) puz-ing. 11) astounding. 12) shocking. 13) infuriating.) worrying. 15) terrifying.

xercise 101
) hurt. 2) upset. 3) flattered. 4) scared. 5) embar-ssed. 6) ashamed. 7) depressed. 8) cheerful.) timid. 10) shy.

xercise 102
) angrily. 2) bravely. 3) greedily. 4) gently.) brightly. 6) well. 7) slowly. 8) sincerely.) badly. 10) wonderfully.

xercise 103
) angrily. 2) gently. 3) greedily. 4) slowly.) wearily. 6) distinctly. 7) securely. 8) carefully.) clumsily. 10) hard.

xercise 104
Would you *like* some milk? No thanks. I'm not irsty. 2) *Would* you *like* a biscuit? Yes please. Would *you like* some toast? No thanks. I'm *not* ingry. 4) *Would you like* a chocolate? *No thanks.* I've *t* toothache. 5) *Would you like* a fire in your room? No anks. I don't feel *cold.*

xercise 105
c. 2) a. 3) b. 4) e. 5) d.

xercise 106
No thanks. I'm *not* hungry. I'd *rather* have a cigar-e. 2) *Would you like* a lift in my car? No *thanks.* I'm *t* tired. I'd *rather* walk. 3) *Would you like* a glass of ilk? No *thanks.* I'm *not* thirsty. I'd *rather have* a ocolate. 4) I'd *sooner* work on a farm *than* in an fice. 5) What *would you rather* do, have a picnic or go a restaurant? 6) I'd *rather* have a picnic.

xercise 107
Shall I close it for you? 2) Shall I get you something eat? 3) Shall I turn on the TV for you? 4) Shall I swer it? 5) Shall I put out the light?

xercise 108
Could you close the window, please? 2) Could you t me something to eat? 3) Could you turn on the V? 4) Could you answer it for me, please? 5) Could u put out the light, please? *B. 'Can you' may be used in all examples.*

xercise 109
Would you mind showing me the way to the Post fice? 2) Would you mind taking my aunt to hospital? Would you mind helping me carry my suitcase?

4) Would you mind smoking outside? 5) Would you mind changing the table-cloth for a clean one?

Exercise 110
1) May I leave the table, please? 2) Please may I watch TV? 3) May I play in the garden, please? 4) May I go upstairs, please? 5) Please may I take the dog for a walk? *N.B. 'Can I' may be used in all examples, and 'please' may go at the beginning or the end of the question – either position is correct.*

Exercise 111
1) Shall we go water-skiing? . . . Then what about playing basket-ball?
Shall we go surfing? . . . Then what about having a picnic?
Shall we have an icecream? . . . Then what about going to a café?
Shall we lie down on the sand? . . . Then what about going for a run?
2) Shall we have some champagne? . . . Then let's have a glass of beer.
Shall we go by taxi? . . . Then let's walk.
Shall we buy some caviar? . . . Then let's buy some sardines.
Shall we stay at a first-class hotel? . . . Then let's stay in a caravan.

Exercise 112
1) What's the matter with George? He's got toothache.
2) What's wrong with the bike? It's got a puncture.
3) What's the matter with the boss? He's lost his temper.
4) What's the matter with you? I've got a cold.
5) What's wrong with the radio? It's got no batteries.

Exercise 113
Shall I; I'd rather; Would you like to; mind if; Can I have; course; would you like to; I'd like; sorry; you mind; Would you like; May I have; would you mind; sorry. Shall I; Excuse me, can I have; I'm afraid; Do you mind; I'm afraid; Would you mind; I'm afraid.

Exercise 114
1) He offers to take the lady's coat. 2) Because she feels cold. 3) By the window. 4) Some soup. 5) Mush-room soup. 6) Because it's cold. 7) Because she has forgotten to bring her purse and has no money. 8) He makes her help him do the washing-up.

Exercise 115
1) the shoe department. 2) the first floor. 3) a pair of boots. 4) She prefers real leather to imitation leather. 5) size six. 6) are very comfortable (they fit her per-fectly). 7) have the same colour. 8) pay by cheque. 9) the boots are cheap. 10) offers to wrap them up.

Exercise 116
2) aren't we? 3) wasn't it? 4) were you? 5) do you? 6) doesn't it? 7) didn't you? 8) did he? 9) aren't I? 10) won't you? 11) will you? 12) hadn't you? 13) can't they? 14) wouldn't you? 15) have you? 16) don't they? 17) don't they? 18) isn't it? 19) Surely? 20) Surely? 21) do they?

126

Exercise 117

1) A private call. 2) Because she has lost her keys.
3) Because the line is engaged. 4) Mr Carter. 5) At a
business meeting. 6) You have to make a appointment. 7) No he doesn't. 8) To take a message.
9) Because they are away. 10) To get the keys sent to
her house.

Exercise 118

1) an appointment . . . suit . . . convenient. 2) speak
. . . in . . . a message . . . phone (ring) back. 3 extension
. . . Hold . . . put you through. 4) urgent . . . reverse
the charges. 5) to have troubled you. 6) you've got the
wrong number.

Exercise 119

1) Can I speak to Mrs James please? 2) Is Cathy in
3) Yes please; I'm sorry to trouble you. 4) Thanks ver
much. 5) All right, thank you. How are you? 6) I'r
sorry to hear that. When will Cathy be back? 7) Shall
ring her back then? 8) Can I leave her a message
(Could you give her a message, please?) 9) Ask her t
ring me at my office tomorrow. 10) I'd like to kno
what day would suit her for the tennis match
11) Thanks a lot. I'm sorry to have troubled you.

ndex